Big things happen in Texas, but there's nothing quite like a West Texas tornado, especially to a small child living through it for the first time. I was just four years old and I remember my father waking me in the middle of the night, wrapping me in a blanket and picking me up in his strong arms. "Don't cry, Marcie. We're just going down in the basement of the store until the weather gets better." I laid my head on his powerful shoulders. I felt, if I could hold onto him forever, I would always be safe.

Once I was tucked away into a corner, Daddy helped others down those stairs to safety. That's the way it was in Texon, neighbors helping each other as if we were all one big family. We were poor, but we didn't know it; everyone was poor.

Growing up in a Texas oil camp was an experience. Everywhere we looked there were oil rigs and the smell of oil. The noise and hum the pumps made as they pulled oil to the tanks were, at first, horrid. But one day I just didn't hear them anymore and, strangely enough, I miss them.

Yes, Texon was more than the smell of an oil camp. It was such a special place that I would wish many times that I could have lived there forever. Many of you know what I mean about the place you grew up, don't you? Now, **TEXAS GOLD** brings Texon back to life.

Joyce Shaughnessy

TEXAS GOLD

Growing up in a Texas oil camp

by

JOYCE SHAUGHNESSY

Swan Publishing
Texas ❖ California ❖ New York

Author: Joyce Shaughnessy
Editors: Pete Billac and Headlee A. Partin
Layout Design: Sharon Davis
Cover Design: Kenneth George

Other Works by Joyce Shaughnessy:

The Long Way Home (Due December 1996)

Copyright @ August 1996
Joyce Shaughnessy
Library of Congress # 96-69148
ISBN# 0-943629-24-1

All rights to this book are reserved. No part may be reproduced or translated by any means, electronic or mechanical, including photocopying, recording, or by any information, storage or receival system without written permission from the author and publisher.

TEXAS GOLD is available in quantity discounts through: Swan Publishing, 126 Live Oak, Alvin, TX 77511. (713) 388-2547 or FAX (713) 585-3738.

Printed in the United States of America.

DEDICATION

I would like to dedicate this work
to my family for all their love and support;
to Doctor Robert Rothstein for his assistance; and
to Mr. Pete Billac for his patience, kindness,
and belief in a new author.

PREFACE

I'm the publisher of this book. Before reading it I felt it necessary to tell you something about it and also why I agreed to publish an unknown author such as Joyce Shaughnessy. Mainly, because the story was good. I read dozens of manuscripts a week and few make it past the first several pages, maybe the first chapter. But this book, TEXAS GOLD, held my interest throughout, and it isn't necessarily "my kind" of reading.

As I write this, I have never met Joyce Shaughnessy other than through telephone conversations, faxed information about the book and her manuscript. But I sincerely know her. You will too as you turn these pages and grow up in the same family as Marcie, Annie and Cheryl. I promise, you'll laugh, cry, sigh and smile at these three young girls as seen through the baby sister's eyes.

It's a wonderful story about growing up that parents would want their children to read. It talks about family and family values, about spirituality, heartache and hard work and the undeniable love their parents had for their three girls.

Each parent loved their children differently but just as completely. Their mother showed her love with visible affection and care. Their father by having a plan to make a better life for them and they succeeded.

In fact, Joyce first named the book A MAN OF QUIET DETERMINATION, a fitting description of her father. Since her fondest memories are the years they spent in Texon, a West Texas oil camp, we thought to call it A SPECIAL PLACE CALLED TEXON. The title we now have, TEXAS GOLD, tells little of what the book is about but as you read along and live life with this family, you'll discover that TEXAS GOLD is what they had all along; they just weren't aware of it.

I hope each of you enjoys this book as much as I have. I think it has an excellent chance to be made into a movie. It's every bit as good a story as LITTLE WOMEN.

And I will encourage Joyce Shaughnessy to complete her second book, perhaps a third and a fourth. I feel she is a gifted writer with depth and dignity. You'll know what I mean as you read this book.

Pete Billac
Publisher

> "For man sees only what is visible,
> but the Lord sees into the heart."
>
> 1 Samuel 16:7

One

"Cheryl, you and Annie have to look after Marcie for me. If she's not crawling out the front door, she's trying to find a spoon to eat dirt. I'm holding you responsible. I have to go. Daddy needs help in the fields."

My mother was always making Cheryl and Annie look after me. In some ways, I guess it wasn't fair to them, but as I once read somewhere, "You play 'em as you get 'em."

I don't remember much about the farm where I was born because we moved when I was only eighteen months old. My parents were peanut farmers on the same land where his father and his grandfather had farmed. Daddy had done his best to make the farm profitable, but the weather and the economy wouldn't cooperate.

I knew we were poor because my sisters told me about living there. They said the house didn't have any paint; the wind and rain had stripped it to bare wood and it was brown with age. We lived on a dusty road close to Blanket, Texas, and dust just seemed to stick to it. We didn't have any inside facilities but, I didn't remember that.

"*Cheryl Elaine*, get out of bed and get dressed for school! You're going to be late again." My mother always had trouble getting Cheryl up in the winter because it was usually *very* cold and the warm blankets were difficult to leave. Too, Cheryl absolutely hated having to go to the outhouse.

The same scenario took place each morning; Cheryl would ignore Mother's entreaties until she used two names. Then, Cheryl would literally vault from the bed because she knew that if she was late for school, my father would know about it. He was already in the fields, but if Cheryl wasn't waiting for the school bus when it came along, he would want to know why.

My father's name was Edward Glenn Fitzgerald. He was 5'11" and kind of stocky. Although only in his early forties, his skin was reddened and wrinkled from working in the sun. His hair was dark brown and thick, and his striking blue eyes remained with you for a long time. My first memories of him are of his coming into the house and kissing my mother like he hadn't seen her for days. Then he would always wash his hands and sit for dinner. Daddy was gruff and to the point. He never said very much, but when he did, there was no doubt that he meant it. Perhaps my father's quiet side naturally evolved from his solitary work on the farm.

Both my parents were determined that their daughters would receive a college education. Like most parents, they didn't want their children spending the rest of their lives struggling to make a meager living, as they had.

☆ ☆ ☆ ☆ ☆ ☆ ☆ ☆ ☆

Daddy managed to keep the farm alive during the depression and on through World War II. His brother, Robert, enlisted in the Air Force. He married in San Francisco just before being shipped overseas. His other brother, Charles, had some sort of mental problem and when he was old enough to leave the farm, he moved to San Antonio. Nobody talked about it, so I don't know much, only that Daddy stayed home and worked the farm. He quit school after the eighth grade. He had no choice.

Uncle Robert, came home after the war with his bride, my Aunt May, and enrolled in college. Daddy tried his best to send money to my uncle Robert at school and to keep the family fed. Mother said that Daddy waited until he was forty to marry so that he could take care of his parents and help put Uncle Robert through school.

☆ ☆ ☆ ☆ ☆ ☆ ☆ ☆ ☆

Mothers' name was Emma Braddock. She was born in Comanche, only about 30 miles from the farm. Her hair was auburn, her eyes were a bright hazel and she was slender. She was also extremely stubborn.

When I was nine years old, my mother told me how she met Daddy; at a dance where his band was playing. He played the fiddle. I even found an old picture of the band and my mother was in it. It's hard for me to imagine that Mother was even allowed to go to dances. Her real father and her stepfather were both Baptist ministers, and dancing was forbidden.

Mother said, "Your father is 11 years older than me but he was so sweet and so handsome. When I went to hear his band play, it wasn't for the music, it was to see him! He was the only one I was interested in, so I just sat and listened to the music. I had to sneak out of the house to go."

"My parents liked him. We met at Sunday services at the Baptist Church in Comanche, so I suppose my parents considered him to be responsible and faithful to the Church. He loved music, and his band played at dances to earn extra money." She smiled happily when telling me how they first met.

Yes, Mother said she had never met anyone that was

so considerate and thoughtful. "And, he had the prettiest blue eyes. I fell in love at first sight because of his eyes. The rest of him just followed."

☆ ☆ ☆ ☆ ☆ ☆ ☆ ☆ ☆

My sister, Cheryl, was born in 1940, and my other sister, Annie, was born in 1944. I was the baby of the family. I came along kind of late in my parents' lives, in 1950, and they named me Marcie. Cheryl wanted to name me Betty Jo after a character in her school reader. Luckily, my mother didn't like that name.

I found another picture of Cheryl and Annie, when Annie was two. In the picture Cheryl is wearing big thick glasses because she has had poor eyesight her entire life. She has her hand around Annie and her mouth open in surprise because the photographer told her to put her arm around her little sister. Most photographers and most strangers thought Annie was a little boy.

Annie was bald until she was almost four, and when her hair did come in, it was stark white, so she still looked kind of bald. My mother said maybe that was one of the reasons Annie decided to be such a tomboy—everyone called her a little boy anyway. I am happy to report, however, that Annie does have a full head of hair now and does not look like a boy; she's beautiful.

My problem and the subject of my family's frustration with me when I was a baby was my personal quest for the perfect tasting *dirt!* It was easy to find several variations of dirt in West Texas, especially on an isolated farm on a dirt road. My mother said that if I could find a spoon, I could find dirt. I should have been a Washington reporter. There's a lot of dirt to uncover there, too.

It was always my mother who talked and told us stories. Daddy never said anything, unless he deemed it important and necessary. We have a picture of my father and Uncle Robert when Daddy was about eight years old, and my uncle must have been about two. Neither were smiling. I remember but a few times when Daddy ever did smile, unless he couldn't help it. My mother once told me that people often thought it was undignified to smile for pictures. For some reason, my father always felt the need to be serious when discussing personal or family matters, like why I enjoyed dirt so much, why Annie was bald, and why peanut farming wasn't more profitable?

My Uncle Robert fought in both World War II and the Korean War. We were all proud of him. He was our family hero. And Daddy, probably every bit the hero too, stayed home and took care of the rest of the family which included two sisters, one other brother, and his parents. Now that I think about it that took a great deal of courage in itself.

☆ ☆ ☆ ☆ ☆ ☆ ☆ ☆ ☆

It was during the war that Daddy's mother died, so I never met her. I have never even seen a picture of her. Mother said she died of a fever. Doctors weren't easy to find, and the money to pay them was scarce.

On one of the rare days that Daddy talked, I remember him telling me about the band he and Uncle Robert had. I suppose they must have had other men in the band, or it technically couldn't be called a band with only two musicians. Daddy played the fiddle and Uncle Robert the base violin. They did it to make extra money, so when Uncle Robert went overseas, Daddy found some fellow farmers who needed the money, and they continued to play at local dances in the area.

It wasn't difficult to find poor farmers in those days, and I don't think it was very hard to please anyone with their musical skills. Any entertainment was welcome through the depression and the war.

When Uncle Robert came back from the war with Aunt May, he was stationed in South Texas, and decided to go to college. Daddy was still working the farm and taking care of the family by himself. I often wondered if Daddy ever resented not seeing any more of the world, or not being able to go to college, but he never said so, at least not to me. He wouldn't have. It wasn't like him to complain.

I have often thought how much easier it would have been for Daddy had we been born boys, you know, to help run the farm. That was never mentioned, just my thoughts. Yes, Daddy was as much a hero as was Uncle Robert. He sacrificed his life for his family.

Like most parents, Mother and Daddy wanted us to have better lives than they had. But it was highly unlikely, almost fantasy, during the 1940's and 1950's for a peanut farmer to even *dream* of sending his children to college. Back then, boys did the same work as their folks and girls were housewives and helped in the fields. But Daddy was hell bent on *his* girls getting a formal education. We knew that Daddy loved us. We all just wished he'd say so now and then.

We always knew how much Mother loved us, because she told us so often. But it was different with Daddy; he seemed like the neighbor who happened to stop by for dinner, only making occasional comments. My father never was one to kiss or hug any of us. The only person we ever saw him kiss and hug was my mother, and there was absolutely no doubt in our minds that he adored her.

Mother told me that Annie and I looked just like her mother and brothers, with blonde hair and blue eyes, and that

Cheryl looked just like my Grandmother Fitzgerald, a brunette with the same blue eyes. I had blond hair and blue eyes just like Annie. The only different physical trait I possessed was really big dimples, and I soon learned to use them to my advantage.

At the end of the Korean war, my uncle hadn't been discharged, my father's band wasn't bringing in much money, and peanut farming was not very profitable. My father sold a piece of our land to an oil company to drill a well but the well didn't produce. It was then my parents decided that peanut farming was not going to provide us with some sort of better life, so we moved to Texon, Texas.

Two

I can only imagine the shock my family must have experienced when they had their first glimpse of West Texas, especially Texon. Large, smelly oil rigs replaced trees, and dust and dirt replaced grass and water. The few trees there were mesquite, more like bushes. Mesquite is maybe three feet high, and just a mess of branches that are ugly and thorny with no leaves. Huge tumbleweeds roared down the street and gained speed the harder the wind blew.

Texon was the embodiment of what had long been termed the "dust bowl" of the country. There were also big, black, hairy tarantulas. I can remember taking bets as we drove the 30 miles from Texon to Big Lake, as to how many of these giant spiders we would spot crossing the road.

Everyone who lived there worked for the oil company except us. One of the earliest and biggest oil gushes in Texas occurred in Texon sometime around the depression. The oil company that owned the land built a park, a school, a church, post office, a small cafe´ with a soda fountain, and the grocery store that my parents operated.

Most of the houses were small. Every house had approximately the same floor plan and was made of white painted wood and heated by a central wood burning heater in the living room. Each house looked pretty much like the next one, like an army camp. And there were railroad tracks almost in our back yard that took the crude oil to refineries in Houston and Galveston.

I know all of this sounds absolutely depressing to most people, but what West Texas, especially Texon, lacked in scenery was quickly replaced by the attitude of the people who lived there. We were all like one large family, each parent taking care of whatever child happened to be in their house that afternoon. There was no class distinction; everyone was poor, some more than others.

When we first moved from the farm, they said I cried for two weeks and never stopped until Mother hung a picture on the living room wall, The tale is that I said, "Good. Now we're home." I don't know if it's true, but it's a good line anyway.

My father and mother were in charge of running the only grocery and dry goods store in Texon. It belonged to a friend of my parents in Rankin who knew my father needed a job and suggested he try his hand at being a shopkeeper. Mother was a bit concerned over this move because Daddy was not outgoing and definitely not a "people" person.

Our new home was several rooms attached to the back of the store. We could enter it either from two separate entrances or through a third door in the back of the store. That door led into my parents' bedroom. And, there was a pool hall between our store and the post office. We kind of lived on Main Street.

Big Lake Oil Company Camp at Texon in 1928.

☆ ☆ ☆ ☆ ☆ ☆ ☆ ☆ ☆ ☆

    Daddy had to make a monumental change in his demeanor. He was forced to become more outgoing, even talkative at times, in order to sell things. He soon learned that customers wanted to be waited on by someone who smiled and conversed. But when he came to the back of the store, to our house, he was the same ole Daddy, quiet and talking only when he deemed necessary.
    He was the butcher and my mother was the cashier.

He was the butcher and my mother was the cashier. One side of the store contained the food stuff and the butcher counter was to the rear of the store. The other side was for the dry goods. I liked that side best. I loved to visit because there were always pictures of dresses in the pattern book and interesting things with which to play.

I was definitely the most prissy of my sisters. I liked colors and lace more than Cheryl and Annie. What I mean is I didn't like Cheryl and Annie *less* than colors and lace, well, you know what I mean.

Mother cut the material people bought and sold patterns, buttons, and thread. Since Mother was around all of that, she felt competent enough to sew for us. She wasn't! My mother, without a doubt, was one of the *worst* seamstresses in Texas! We would cringe every time she offered to make us something, especially when it was out of scraps she had left in the store. Do you have any idea what it's like to go to school with a patchwork skirt that doesn't fit and looks like the map of Texas?

We prayed for hand-me-downs from our cousins in San Antonio and Uncle Robert's wife, Aunt May, sewed beautifully. We only got two new store-bought dresses a year—one for Easter, which was reserved for church, and one for school. I would still rather wear the same dress to school every day than wear something my mother made for me.

As time passed, Daddy talked more to the customers, but still, not much changed in our house in that area. My mother was the one who punished us and taught us how she thought we should behave. If something profound happened, both of my parents would sit with us for a discussion, but Daddy would just kind of shake his head and nod, then get up and go back to the store.

The only subject I can remember my father talking to

us about was our education, and he always looked at our report cards. If we had anything on them that he didn't like, he would ground us and make us work extra in the store.

☆ ☆ ☆ ☆ ☆ ☆ ☆ ☆ ☆

Texon turned out to be a wonderful place to live. Although we were literally surrounded by oil rigs and the smell they discharged, we couldn't have cared less. We got so accustomed to it that when anyone came for a visit and commented on the horrible smell, we were actually surprised. We never even noticed it.

About two hundred people lived in Texon; it was like one huge family. We liked having people around us. My mother was pleased with the move because she was outgoing and friendly; she enjoyed talking to the customers as they shopped. And, I think she worried less about us because each family knew the other families.

There was a big park in the middle of the camp which was everyone's responsibility to maintain. I loved it because the adults planted big, beautiful trees and lots of flowers. Just outside the camp, within eyesight of every street, were the messy oil rigs, but inside the camp was neat and clean. When I think back, Texon was the happiest time for my family, not just for me. It was a special and wonderful place to live.

I know Cheryl loved Texon because she made a lot of friends her age. Annie loved it for the same reason, but also because it was a perfect setting for her to stir things up a bit. Annie was full of mischief. I think she must have been that way since birth. Texon offered her a larger and more interesting territory on which to embark on her quest for adventure, and it usually involved me. Annie became my heroine because she always had so much fun.

No matter how much she strived to get rid of me, it hardly worked. I was stubborn and willful, too. If we had stayed in Texon, I probably would have become just like Annie, mischievous and always looking for adventure around the next corner. Even now, I know that Annie is searching for her next escapade.

☆ ☆ ☆ ☆ ☆ ☆ ☆ ☆

"Mommy," I whined, "Annie won't let me play with her." I was a terrific whiner, probably the best in Texon.

"I'll talk to her as soon as I have a chance," Mother said, then went about her business. Annie knew how to hide from me, but I had other things to do, like my personal quest for different kinds of dirt. They told me that I was the dirt-finding champion of all time,

I'd look for Annie and if I couldn't find her, I'd grab a spoon and head for the living room. We didn't have carpet; the floors were hardwood. But, the dirt in the house was definitely tastier than outside dirt, and I knew my dirt. House dirt *always* had a better flavor than outside dirt; maybe it had something to do with the polish mixed in with it or the fact that it didn't have the smell of oil. The doctor told mother that the dirt wouldn't hurt me and that lots of kids ate dirt.

Mother said I would rather eat dirt than anything else. She said I just crawled around with a spoon or whatever was handy and would dig dirt between the boards on the floor of the house. Everyone who lived in Texas knows that no matter how much you sweep, mop, and clean, dirt will collect everywhere, and apparently, at that age, I foresaw a huge accumulation of tantalizing delights.

One day, when I was dutifully searching with a spoon for dirt to eat, Annie came striding in the house. The first words out of her mouth were, "I'm going to tell Mother that you're eating dirt again, and you're going to get into so much trouble!" I replied with as much sarcasm as a four-year-old can muster, "Go ahead. She knows I eat dirt, and she doesn't care."

"Oh yeah? Well, I heard Mother tell Aunt Bessie that the doctor was testing you for *pinworms* because you were eating so much dirt. He said that if you had pinworms, you would have to take the most awful, foul and putrid smelling medicine ever invented for human consumption and would probably have to get a hysterectomy!"

Annie could sometimes come up with big words! I didn't know what many of them meant but she made them sound decidedly important and awful.

"Oh yeah? You're just jealous because Mommy pays more attention to me than to you. I like dirt."

Unfortunately, Annie was absolutely right. The doctor called my mother and said she had to come into town to pick up medicine, the kind that Annie said tasted so awful. But guess what? It was medicine for *the entire family*! And, it was every bit as awful-tasting as Annie said it would be.

My mother tried to disguise the medicine by putting it in Coke or orange juice, but we knew better. The minute she walked into the room with it, we could smell it coming. I wish I remembered the name of that medicine so I would never get it again.

Even Mother and Daddy had to take the medicine. The first time they tried to show us how to take it without making a fuss, they made such horrible faces as it went down that we couldn't help but laugh. Funny, but for the next few weeks, Daddy was a lot harder for Mother to find. He hated that medicine as much as we did.

It actually smelled as if a skunk *lived* in it, and I'm not so sure that it wasn't made out of skunk oil. I was convinced it must have been manufactured by some drug company who sold the medicine to desperate Texans who had children who ate large amounts of dirt. I suppose that's a pretty small market, so I guess pinworms come from other places, too.

The entire family had to be very careful about handwashing all of the time; which didn't sit well with Annie since she was such a tomboy. She climbed every tree and fence she could find and was always dirty. I think she loved the dirt as much as I did. She just didn't eat it.

Neither Annie nor Cheryl ever forgave me for having to take *the medicine!* Annie commented that she would have gladly choked me if she knew she wouldn't get in trouble for it.

☆ ☆ ☆ ☆ ☆ ☆ ☆ ☆ ☆

Any person who has not experienced the cold winter wind in a wooden house with just one stove cannot possibly imagine how cold, *cold* really is. If you faced the fire, you were warm in front but still cold in back. If you moved more than a few feet from the fire it was cold. If someone was standing between you and the fire, it was cold.

As usual, Cheryl had to impress us with her knowledge and experience of discomfort. "You might not remember us having to go *outside* to the bathroom in the winter when we lived on the farm. It was cold inside our house, colder outside when we ran to the outhouse, and when we had to sit in that smelly thing, it was still cold. This is a luxury in comparison."

Still, I recall vividly that there was never enough room close to the stove. I always seemed to be too far back to feel any real heat. I could barely get one good whine out of my mouth before Mother admonished, "Just be quiet, Marcie.

Your daddy has to get up an hour earlier every morning to get things ready in the store. If you want me to, I'll just start waking *you* first to build the fire. Then you'll be first to get close to it."

My mother knew just how to make me shut up, which in itself was an accomplishment considering I had really perfected my whining abilities. The battle over the stove continued every winter until Cheryl and Annie grew up and moved. Each of us tried to wake up ahead of the others to get close to the stove for warmth while dressing. It became first there, first warmed.

In summer, when it was hot outside, it was hotter inside, so we played outside most of the time. I don't think any of knew what an air conditioner was, but we did have a large window fan in the kitchen. But, I swear, I think it only *sucked* hot air from the outside then sort of *threw it* at you.

☆ ☆ ☆ ☆ ☆ ☆ ☆ ☆ ☆ ☆

The first birthday party I can remember was my fourth. I was dressed in my cowboy suit, complete with guns, hat, and a stick horse. I wanted to be Roy Rogers. Annie informed me that I would have to be Dale Evan because I was a girl, but I ignored her. Everyone knew that Roy Rogers was smarter and braver than Dale Evans—he just let her hang around to help him with the singing. Besides, I wasn't sure if Dale Evans wore pants or a skirt, and I wanted to wear pants because of all the tumbleweeds. When they hit you on the legs, they really stung.

In one of my birthday pictures is the black and white dog Annie found and brought home. I remember how she came bounding in the back door, dirty as usual, but exceptionally nice to everyone—especially Mother. She finally blurted out, "Mom, what if you saw a dog that was abandoned and hungry, would you take care of it?"

Mother knew what was coming, "Of course I would. I would bring it home, feed it, then take it back to where I found it. Texon isn't very big, Annie, so I'm sure the real owner is out looking for the dog."

"But, Mom, I know it doesn't belong to anybody. It's all skinny and dirty. Besides, she's already in the back yard, and she's so sweet. Please, *please* can I have her?"

"Let's go look at it. I'm not saying "yes" but if we keep it, under no circumstances does it set foot in this house."

The whole family went out to look. The dog was friendly and wagged it's tail and came over to let each of us pet her. She looked neglected. There's no doubt it was abandoned.

Mother said we would post a sign in the store for a week, then if the dog wasn't claimed, since Annie found her, Annie was to take care of her. Of course, Annie swore she would. She named the dog "Spots" because it was covered with black and white spots. Daddy said it was okay as long as if Annie fed her.

Every night Daddy would make sure that Spots was inside the fence so she couldn't get hurt or run off, and Annie, as she promised she would, fed her and gave her a weekly bath with the water hose. About a week after my 5th birthday, something happened that was traumatic and painful for all of us. I'll never forget it.

In our area of Texas, people either worked in the oil business or did sheep ranching. One day a pack of wild dogs killed some sheep. The owner of the ranch where the sheep were killed came into Texon with looking for dogs. Spots was asleep in our front yard, and the rancher knocked on the door.

My father answered the knock."My name is Tom Warren. I own a sheep ranch just northeast of here, and I would like for your family to come out in the front yard so that I can show them something."

Daddy made me stay inside, but I saw what went on outside from the living room window. Daddy, Mother, Annie and Cheryl went outside with Mr. Warren.

Mr. Warren went to his truck and took a shotgun from the front seat. Mother, Daddy and my sisters were just standing there, not knowing what to expect. I could see that Mr. Warren was mad.

"I need for all these damned dogs to stay away from my ranch and stop killing my sheep," Mr. Warren said. Before anybody knew what was happening, he raised the shotgun to his shoulder, pointed it at Spots, and pulled the trigger.

I couldn't believe it! Cheryl and Annie began screaming and crying and Annie went up to Spots, knelt down and held her in her arms. Spots was dead.

Mother grabbed Annie and took her and Cheryl inside immediately. I saw Daddy's face redden, his eyes squint and his jaw set. "You are a mean person, Mr. Warren. Our Spots never leaves this yard. Get out of my sight. If you ever set foot on this property again, I'll do to you what you did to poor Spots. In fact, you'd better be gone when I come back because I'm going for *my* gun. And when I come out it won't be some innocent, defenseless dog I'll be shooting."

Daddy turned around, walked into the house, and got his rifle. Mother started crying. "Edward, please just leave it alone. Please!"

"Emma, I love you and the girls more than anything on this earth, and that's precisely why I'm going out there now. He's some sort of animal, doing that in front of my girls. I want to make sure he doesn't do it anymore, anywhere." With that, Daddy walked out the front door as Mr. Warren burned rubber getting away.

It was maybe ten minutes before Daddy came back inside the house. He was still mad but his face wasn't as red. He hung his loaded rifle back on the wall in the living room and picked up the telephone and placed a call to the sheriff in Big Lake.

"Sheriff, tell that Warren guy this matter isn't over. Tell him if I ever set eyes on him again, I'll shoot him like a rattler." I don't know what the sheriff told Daddy but the conversation ended when Daddy repeated, "Don't forget to tell him what I said, sheriff," and Daddy hung up the phone.

Cheryl and Annie stopped crying while Daddy was talking to the sheriff but when he hung up, they started in again. By then, I was crying, too.

Then Daddy sat with us in the living room. "I know I lost my temper out there girls, and I know that probably isn't a very good example for you, but a man like Mr. Warren is liable to do anything to anyone. What he just did was downright cruel and heartless. Not everybody's like that, thank the Lord."

That was the longest Daddy had probably ever spoken to us. "Sometimes you just have to stand up for yourself," Daddy continued. " If you treat people right and they still have the nerve to do what Mr. Warren did, then you have to show him you're just as strong as they are. The only thing that made Mr. Warren so brave was the fact that he had a gun. That's cowardice, not bravery. Someday that Warren guy will get what's coming to him. Everyone does. It says so in the Bible."

Daddy then went out. He came back in about an hour, and we were all somewhat calmed down by then. Annie was still crying some.

"I'm sorry about Spots," Daddy told us. "Com'on Annie. He was your dog so let's you and me bury him beside the church."

The next day when Daddy came in the kitchen, we were

all there. "I talked to Mrs. Shearson and she told me that her basset hound was about to have puppies, and said we could have one. Would you like that?" he asked, looking directly at Annie.

Annie wasn't too sure about another dog. She didn't want the same thing to happen. She looked at Mother who seemed to understand her thoughts. She took Annie in her arms, "Annie, if you housebreak this new puppy and keep it inside the gate or in the house, it will be safe." Annie smiled.

"You realize, of course, you'll have to clean up any mistakes it makes. A puppy will be a lot easier to train than Spots was. And Daddy made sure Mr. Warren or anybody like him wouldn't hurt our dog. Word spreads fast."

About two months later, Daddy came home with the little puppy, whose ears were as big as his body. Annie was thrilled. She took the pup from Daddy and wrapped her arms around it, holding it close to her body. She named him "Sad Sack" from the comic strips because he always looked sad as basset hounds do.

The sheriff had that talk with Mr. Warren and told him what Daddy said. But that didn't stop the cruelty. Mr. Warren and the other sheep ranchers developed a much more ingenious method of killing the dogs; they threw poisoned meat in the yards. Other dogs died and nobody could prove who was doing it, but we knew.

But Sad Sack was safe. Annie kept him in the house almost all of the time, and he lived a long age as a special part of the family. His existence reminded us that Daddy would always take care of us if we needed him.

Daddy showed his strength in other ways too. That same year he went to the doctor in Big Lake because he had been coughing a lot. The doctor told him he needed to quit smoking, so when he got back home, he put the pack of cigarettes he always carried in the top pocket of his shirt, on top of the bureau.

"Emma," he said, "I don't want anyone to move that pack of cigarettes. I want to remember it every time I walk in the door. It'll remind me not to smoke."

My mother didn't move it, and I specifically remember that the same pack was up there when we moved from Texon about eight years later. I never did see my father smoke another cigarette.

☆ ☆ ☆ ☆ ☆ ☆ ☆ ☆ ☆

My mother was Cheryl's girl scout leader when we lived in Texon, so I was allowed to go on all of the troop outings. One of the trips was overnight to a lake around San Angelo. We pitched tents and cooked hot dogs and marshmallows around a campfire. I remember everyone telling scary stories. Mother let me sleep in her tent.

Later that night, we heard some of the girls running from their tents screaming to beat hell because they had heard a noise. My mother told the girls that it was just an owl. She took a flashlight and shined it into the tree, and sure enough, there it was. I must not have been the only person who was scared.

The girl scouts also went on a trip to Carlsbad Caverns. I don't remember that trip at all, but I heard about it for the next four years. Mother said she carried me all the way through the caverns (that was before the caverns had elevators). She said I started crying from the first minute we walked into the caves. She vowed that I would never go on another troop trip. I didn't..

Later the next year, when Mother took the girls on another trip, Daddy and I "batched" it. I thought it was great.

That Friday afternoon, Daddy came in the house to make certain that I had gotten home okay. "Would you like go out tonight and have supper?", he asked. Would I? I quickly yelled, "Yes!" We had never gone out anywhere for supper because we never had the money to spare. It was one of the biggest events in my young life to go *out* and to be in a café, and with Daddy!

Daddy ordered for me. "We would like two hamburgers with french fries and a chocolate shake for Marcie." I loved Daddy for treating me special. It was kind of like having a date. If we went anywhere on any kind of trip, he would buy bologna, a loaf of bread and Miracle Whip. Eating out was something we simply did not do. I remember begging Mother to take the girls on another trip just so Daddy and I could go to the café again.

There were times that my father and I had kind of a special bond. I'm not sure why. Maybe it was because of my dimples or because I was the baby of the family. I was the only one with dimples, and almost always got singled out when I went into the store. Some customer would come in and say, "How are you today? Where did you get those pretty dimples?"

My answer was always the same, "From God." Then the person would usually give me something, like a piece of candy, and then pinch me hard on the cheeks. Sometimes the candy wasn't worth the pinches, but it generally was.

☆ ☆ ☆ ☆ ☆ ☆ ☆ ☆

In Texon, I was always walking around smiling like I knew some private joke, because all of the adults liked my dimples. The people who lived next door to us thought the dimples were really cute, so cute in fact, that I was the only one allowed to pick persimmons off their tree. I used that for leverage for other favors because, the fact was, I didn't even *like* persimmons.

    If Annie were with me she always made fun of me, "What do you think you're doing? You look stupid walking around with that dumb smile on your face all the time." I bet she would have done the same thing if she were the one with the dimples.

    There were times I would slip back into my dirt-eating mode. Whenever I wasn't on my mission to find for the best tasting dirt in town, I was trying to keep the house. Somehow the two things sound contradictory. It astounds me that a four-year-old girl could be as concerned as I was about the cleanliness of her house, but I was. The earliest memories of my childhood involve following my family around and cleaning up after them. There is a saying, "Cleanliness is next to Godliness." If that were true, I must have earned a lot of points with God, except of course, when I was eating dirt.

    I was such a compulsive cleaner that I would hide somewhere just waiting to snap into action. When I was alone, I dusted, swept, mopped, scoured, polished, and put things in their proper places for hours. It was almost like cleanliness was my *calling*. I have always hated messiness, whether it's my house, the office, or my car. It's a surprise to me that I didn't become a motel maid or at least a housekeeper. The "cleaning phase" must be representative of my compulsive perfectionism. It must have driven my family crazy, following them around and making certain that no crumbs were dropped and that everything was kept in its proper order.

    Maybe I should have been born Japanese so that each person removed their shoes when they came in the front door. I have read that the Japanese culture is one of cleanliness, and I would have loved it.

I still have spurts of cleanliness when I'm angry or nervous. I suppose it isn't really too bad a habit. It takes the place of a martini, and it does seem to keep things "under control." I honestly thought I was being useful and providing my family with a sanitary living environment, and all I usually accomplished was irritating everyone. It is my personal belief that every person should have goals to which they aspire. My goal then was to apparently keep things neat and tidy. A psychiatrist once told me that it was a need to keep things in control, and I guess that probably sums it up, although I liked being noticed, too. It was fun being the center of attention. Perhaps that was why Annie always got in trouble. She liked the attention.

I should have been an actress since I had such a tremendous need to be noticed. Annie's goal was much simpler. Her ambition was to make me mad enough to leave her alone, and she almost succeeded.

I was so young at the time, that I didn't realize what Mother and Daddy were trying to accomplish, other than having us live in a Christian home, having enough to eat, and otherwise providing us with what they considered a proper home. I don't think that Annie's escapades were something that my parents appreciated or condoned, but Annie was always an individual with strong convictions. Although she loved my parents as much as Cheryl and I did, she would never allow them to suppress her.

It seemed to me then, that Cheryl's intended purpose in life was to look good and have a lot of dates. Of course, there was more, but when you are only four years old, you don't always catch the hidden agendas. Besides, it was Annie who had to take me everywhere she went. She didn't appreciate it, and she showed it in a million ways.

Three

Annie's mission of revenge began from the first day she had to drink the "skunk oil" medicine. She never forgot that it was my fault that she had to drink it! She didn't start enacting her plans until I was about four. My mother, like thousands of other mothers, always made Annie take me along with her so she could babysit me.

It usually began with, "Mommy, can I please go with Annie and Erin? Oh, please, *pleeeeeeease!*" (Erin was Annie's best friend). Mother usually made her take me along so that I would shut up. Annie was supposed to take care of me, but she was always in trouble. She and Erin would constantly dream up ways to make me whine, cry, or even better, leave them alone.

Erin had emerald green eyes, and pretty blonde hair that she wore in a ponytail. She didn't look like a tomboy, but you can't always tell things by appearances. I'm not sure if it was Annie or Erin who was the bigger troublemaker, but I know that Annie felt her *calling* was to make me the eternal victim! She succeeded, and Erin came along for the ride.

Annie started her objective with the *big barn caper* when I was about four. I was always afraid to try new things, but somehow Annie and Erin managed to talk me into going up on the roof of the barn. *Peter Pan* was the hottest ticket in town. I had a view finder with *Peter Pan* in it and even charged other kids five cents to look at my view finder for ten minutes. Man, I was really cleaning up!

A friend of my mother's whom we called "Aunt Bessie" took me and a friend into Big Lake to see *Peter Pan*. When the man at the ticket counter told Aunt Bessie how much it would cost per ticket, she was so surprised that she said, "*Jesus! Do we get to keep the seats, too?"*

Aunt Bessie was the best part of the trip. She also had a fight with a lady wearing a big hat who was sitting in front of us. She finally made that woman move. No one would mess with Aunt Bessie. She knew her place in life, and if you didn't know yours, she would tell you where it was.

Peter Pan soon became my idol, even more than Roy Rogers and Dale Evans. Anyway, Annie and Erin knew how much I worshiped *Peter Pan*, so they told me that if I jumped off the roof it would make me feel like *Peter Pan*. I could just imagine soaring through the air as gracefully as he did. It was a completely different story, however, when I got up on the roof and saw how far down I would have to jump, I clung to it like a cat.

Annie and Erin were persistent, and after about an hour of trying to convince me to jump, Annie just pushed me off. Well, I didn't soar. I skinned every visible part of my body, and I ran straight to Mother to tell on Annie!

"Mommy! Mommy! Annie hurt me. She pushed me off the roof of the barn! Spank her. It *Huuuurts!* " (Besides being a great whiner I was also a very good tattletale.) I didn't realize that the reason it hurt so much was that I had broken my arm.

"If I catch you pushing Marcie off of *anything* ever again, you'll be grounded for life, and I mean it!", my mother was so angry with Annie that it even scared me, and I hadn't done anything! Daddy had to drive me to the doctor in Big Lake, and he made Annie sit in the back seat. He said he was going to make her sit in the examining room while the doctor set my arm. Although it hurt a lot, it was fun seeing Annie sitting so meekly in the back seat. We didn't see that side of her very often.

My broken arm got a lot of attention, and I made Annie wait on me hand and foot for about a week. That is, until my mother told me to stop. She said she thought Annie had suffered enough.

You would think that constantly getting into trouble and being punished for it would stop Annie from deliberately doing things to me that she knew would eventually get back to Mother or Daddy. But not Annie. She wasn't one to be discouraged easily once she had set her mind upon a target.

One of the meanest tricks she and Erin played on me involved an old man who lived close to the camp. He had a long gray beard and wore dirty overalls all of the time. He looked really mean. I thought he was really, really old—like maybe 50. Once a month he came into the store for supplies. All of the kids in camp referred to him as *the hermit.*

The *hermit* always brought at least three vicious looking dogs with him and tied them to the post across the street. When he finished his shopping, he would untie the dogs and they would follow him home.

Annie and Erin asked me, "Did you see that dirty man with all those dogs this morning? He's a hermit, you know, somebody who lives all by himself out in the middle of nowhere because he hates other people. He hates little kids so much that he has his dogs trained to eat them alive!" My eyes opened as wide as saucers.

Annie said that those dogs could tell from a mile away if there were any kids around, and if they got mad enough, they'd even break the ropes holding them back in order to bite a kid. I was so gullible that I believed every word. I was so terrified of that man that I ran and hid every time he came to town.

Years later, Annie told me that she and Erin would go out to the man's house and play with his dogs. They said the man was really nice and just liked to live by himself. I spent years in terror of that man for nothing! Then I started thinking about all of the afternoons I hid out in our hot living room, and I just got madder! When I told Mother and Daddy what Annie had done, they didn't even care. All they did was laugh. Mother told me to stop whining so much and to go outside and play. The whole world was against me!

Annie and Erin also talked me into one of the dumbest tricks probably ever played on any sister to date. They stacked old boxes from the store and climbed up into the attic while Mother and Daddy were busy in the store. Then Annie went on "search detail" to find me. After she found me, Annie climbed up into the attic with Erin and just sat there waiting for me to walk in and see all those boxes piled up to the ceiling. I finally did come in and asked them what all those boxes were there for, "We used those boxes to climb up because there's a lot of neat stuff up here, like old dresses and hats, but there isn't room enough for three people," Annie added.

Annie knew how much I like to play dress-up. "I guess we could climb down and then you could come up. That way there would be plenty of room for you to play with all of this treasure!"

So Annie and Erin climbed down and helped me climb up. Then they pushed the boxes away, and I was stuck up in that dusty old attic. There wasn't even any neat stuff up there at all. I thought I handled myself really well though. I started crying.

Annie and Erin put all of the boxes back where they found them and then went outside in search of other potential "victims." Daddy came into the house later, heard me crying, saw my legs dangling out of the attic, and knew that Annie must have done something again. He got his ladder, helped me down, and told me to take a bath.

When Annie came waltzing in for dinner, Daddy was sitting there with his belt. "Come here, Annie, and take your punishment. I am sick and tired of you and Erin playing tricks on Marcie." Annie got a spanking, and I thought I would get my revenge, but Annie took the spanking without one tear. I couldn't believe it! I wondered if I would do that when I became older and decided that I probably wouldn't. When I ate dinner, I felt secure in the knowledge that at least Annie and Erin wouldn't be mean to me for a while.

    They waited for about a week, and then played the same game on me when they talked me into climbing one of the big trees in the front yard. I was only four years old, and after the barn incident, I was deathly afraid of heights. I just stayed in the tree, whining and crying for help. One of the neighbors came to my rescue and took me into the store. Annie was in trouble again!

    That same year, my mother took Annie, Cheryl, and me to San Angelo to shop. San Angelo was about fifty times the size of Big Lake, so this was a big deal. We never got to go anywhere as cosmopolitan as San Angelo. The new Sears store had an escalator! I was so impressed by it that all I wanted to do was to ride up and down on it all day long.

    Anyway, Mother put Annie in charge of watching me so she could shop in peace. Annie, of course was not only bored with the whole thing, but also embarrassed about having to babysit a four-year-old who went up and down the escalator. After about fifteen minutes, Annie told me, "You have to be very careful when you get to the top or come to the bottom because the escalator will *suck you in by the toes*! I heard somebody talking about it a while ago, and they said that in New York City, a little kid was riding the escalator, and his whole foot sucked right into the thing and they had to cut off his leg up to the knee! And another little kid in Los Angeles got sucked in when he was five years old, and that was two years ago. They haven't seen him since."

Being the fool I was, I believed her and ran through Sears yelling at the top of my lungs, "Mommy, Mommy, Annie said that the escalator would eat me if I got on it! Help!" I am quite certain that the Sears manager was appreciative of our escapade that day. I continued to believe it because I was so entirely trusting of Annie that I believed everything she told me. I lived in mortal fear of escalators for about two years, until Mother told me it wasn't true. I just wondered how old I had to become before I would learn not to believe everything anybody told me.

One of the more embarrassing tricks Annie played on me involved a trip to the cafe' when I was about five. Again, Mother told Annie to watch over me. This particular trick was carefully orchestrated by Annie and Erin. We went down to the cafe' for cokes in Styrofoam cups. When we were out of range from adults, Annie told me that I had to eat the Styrofoam cup, too. She told me, "Yeah, the people who make the Styrofoam cups say you can just eat the whole thing after you're finished and not have to throw anything away."

It took about half an hour of convincing because I didn't want to eat *anything* I wasn't certain about after the pinworm fiasco. In fact, Annie even had to take a tiny bite herself, to convince me to believe it, so I finally did. I ate my entire Styrofoam cup! I cannot *believe* that I was so stupid. I will *never* live that down. I had a stomachache for about two days. I still refuse to drink from Styrofoam cups. Mother and daddy made Annie sweep the store for a week for that one, but, as usual, it didn't do any good.

My parents kept making things worse; they ordered Annie to teach me to swim. I was terrified of the water—the way that I was terrified of everything else. Poor Annie. I would stand in the shallow end of the pool, screaming at the top of my lungs, "Help me, Annie, HELP ME! I'M DROWNING! I'M

DROWNING!" Here I was yelling about drowning, and the water was only coming up to my knees.

I can't remember when I finally learned to swim. It must have been out of self-preservation. I am positive that after having to listen to my screaming, I alienated every other person in the camp. My screaming was so annoying to everyone within earshot that I was no longer their favorite. I had gone from cute to annoying in one summer. I wonder if they thought I was mentally retarded since the swimming incident came right after the Styrofoam trick.

There was one time though, that Annie and Erin saved my life by preventing me from bleeding to death. Mother and Daddy temporarily lost their minds and left Annie to watch over me all of one *entire* Saturday. They went to San Angelo to do some Christmas shopping. I don't remember where Cheryl was, but she wasn't at home.

Annie and Erin took me over to the playground at the school and actually stayed there while I tried every piece of the playground equipment. God had to have intervened. I was coming down the slide and cut my hand on a place on the slide that was sticking up. It was a really big cut, and I still have the scar to prove it. Annie and Erin rushed me over to Erin's house (because it was closer to the playground than our house). I dripped huge pools of blood all the way over and through Erin's house and on their white carpet. They ran about a gallon of Texon water over the cut and then bandaged it. When my parents came home later than night, the cut had stopped bleeding. Annie and Erin had poured a bottle full of iodine on it afterwards. The doctor said it was a miracle that I hadn't developed gangrene from the amount of Texon water Annie and Erin had run through my cut, but that it was healing remarkably well. Annie was always like that. She would tease me until I cried one day, then save me from dying the next.

Annie also never let anyone else ridicule me. That was a clear invasion of *her* territory. I remember walking down the street to the store, and some of the other kids started calling me, "Goody-Two Shoes." It didn't matter to Annie what I was or that she called me the same thing almost every day. As my older sister, she assumed that ridiculing me was her right, and Annie was very protective of her domain.

I vividly remember her riding her bicycle as fast as she could and yelling at the top of her lungs, "The first one of you I catch, I'll throw off the school bus tomorrow. Leave my sister alone!" She truly scared those little kids. She jumped off her bike and grabbed the first one she could by his collar, "You leave Marcie alone. You hear me? I'll make you *really sorry* if you ever bother her again!" Everyone believed Annie when she promised revenge. They knew she meant it.

I worshiped Annie after that name-calling, school-bus-tossing incident. She pedaled her way into my heart from pest to heroine with one single action. I was never bothered again. There have been many times I wished I possessed Annie's courage and bravado.

Four

Usually, it was Mother who disciplined us because Daddy was always too busy in the store. But there was one time that Annie and Erin got into so much trouble that Daddy had to intervene. If my father got mad enough to punish us, we remembered it!

Next to the store was a pool hall. It was for men only, and the men would openly gamble on pool games. My father never gambled because he didn't approve of it. He never had the money to gamble anyway. One afternoon during the summer when the pool hall was closed and Annie and Erin were bored, they broke a window in the side of the building, went in, and played a few games of pool. I think their motive was also to find a building with at least one good air conditioner. They did it a lot, Annie later told me.

While Annie was in the process of climbing through the window, she tore the only pair of blue jeans she owned. I'm sure she was upset because that meant she wouldn't get another pair, and that Mother would patch them with a scrap from the store that definitely wouldn't match..

My guess is that Annie and Erin thought my parents would never find out who broke into the pool hall. I still can't believe they didn't get caught earlier, considering the fact that the pool hall was between the store and the post office, and they left their bikes parked by the windows. Instead of going back through the broken window and riding off on their bicycles, they actually had the nerve to unlock the door from the inside and walk out.

Annie told me later than she and Erin had also found some beer, and both of them had drunk two each. Annie was 11 then. I don't know if that was the truth or just bluster; however, it might be the reason why they didn't have the good sense to go back through the broken window.

Miss Early, the postmistress, happened to be walking by when Annie and Erin walked out of the pool hall. There could not have been a worse person to see them. Miss Early was one of the nosiest people in town. I guess maybe it was from glancing at everyone's mail. I have no doubt that she read every single postcard before putting it in the appropriate box. It wouldn't have surprised me in the least to discover that she steamed open the envelopes.

In Texon, our mail wasn't delivered to mailboxes in front

of our houses, but was put into different boxes in the post office building. Miss Early practically *sprinted* to the store so she could drop this latest bombshell on my mother.

"Emma, Emma, guess who I just saw walking out of the pool hall? It was Annie and Erin. Those two will do anything. Nobody else was there, Mr. Stephens is out of town, so they must have broken in. You poor thing, having to put up with Annie's antics all of the time."

The look on my mother's face was probably good for at least two weeks worth of gossip. However, with as much dignity as she could muster, she put Miss Early in her place, "I'm proud of Annie. She's just a little high-spirited, that's all. Edward and I will take care of this. Thank you for the information." Then Mother walked to the back of the store to inform Daddy of what Annie had done. My father told Mother that he would handle this one.

He went outside, found Annie and Erin, and made them sit in the living room while he walked over to Erin's house to find her mother. While they were being interrogated, Annie and Erin were stupid enough to admit that they were gambling and having a good time the entire three hours they were playing pool. They didn't admit that they had been drinking beer though. They weren't that dumb.

There are so many sins available to a good Southern Baptist to commit, like dancing, lying, being envious of others, etc., but breaking and entering was absolutely *sacrilege* besides being illegal. And gambling on top of that! Annie and Erin were really in for it. Because of the seriousness of their crimes, my father was absolutely *furious!* Not only had Annie and Erin done something he believed to be wrong, he was also faced with calming my mother down, who was certain that such a horrible sin would cause them to live forever in the fires of Hell!

Daddy grounded Annie for a month and gave her a hard spanking with his belt. Then the two sets of parents had to decide who would pay for the broken window. Daddy offered, "I will pay for the window, but Annie has to sweep out the store every day for a month, and Erin will have to clean the front windows every other day for a month." Erin's mother agreed, and Annie and Erin served their time.

Annie and Erin never again broke into a building. They decided it was fun, but not that much fun. And, it caused so much trouble. Both sets of parents considered forbidding the girls to play together, but that was impractical, considering the size of Texon. Erin's parents thought Annie was the bad influence, and I think it probably *was* Annie who dreamed up the whole scheme. There was one thing for certain you could say about Annie; she was adventurous, and she wasn't afraid of anything, except for maybe Cheryl.

☆ ☆ ☆ ☆ ☆ ☆ ☆ ☆ ☆

One day, Cheryl decided she would apply her makeup skills and transform Annie from a tomboy to a glamorous woman, all in one afternoon. I don't think Annie really wanted to try it, but I suppose she decided it was easier to go along with Cheryl than to fight her over it. After all, it had only been two or three weeks since she had broken into the pool hall, and she was still in trouble over that. I guess maybe Annie also reasoned that Mother and Daddy might finally overlook the entire "pool hall caper" if she looked more grown up and glamorous. One thing was certain, Annie didn't want to cause any more waves around the house for a while.

Well, Cheryl started her make over about one o'clock in the afternoon. The hair part was quite simple and going well. However, the makeup part wasn't as successful. Cheryl used her eyelash curler on Annie's right eye, only she forgot to put the *curler pads* and the curler cut all of the eyelashes off! To this day, her right eyelash has never grown back like her left. You could have heard Annie screaming a mile away! "HOW COULD YOU BE SO STUPID? DON'T EVER TOUCH MY BODY AGAIN!"

I got into trouble, too, just because of sitting on the bed watching. Cheryl told Mother that I was talking the whole time, and she got distracted. Yeah, RIGHT! I just happened to be in the wrong place at the wrong time. I personally don't think Cheryl felt too remorseful over the situation. Mother punished Cheryl by grounding her for the weekend and not letting her do any more makeovers on Annie. BIG DEAL! Cheryl was probably too intimidated by her recent mishap that she didn't want to have anything to do with makeups on either Annie or me.

That year I managed to get myself into trouble without Cheryl or Annie's help. Mother was always scolding me for not taking the gum out of my mouth before I took a nap. I forgot one day, and when I woke up, my gum was firmly meshed into my hair. I knew Mother was going to say something like, "I told you so." It is my **firm conviction** that there isn't a child alive who doesn't absolutely dread that phrase. The only solution I could think of was to cut the gum out. The problem was, I had to cut a big chunk out of the front left side of my hair. I didn't think Mother would notice. Obviously, she did, but didn't get angry. She just said, "I told you so." Just like Annie's eyelashes that never grew back, my hair didn't either. It has been thinner on that side ever since.

One of the few things Annie and I agreed upon was that Cheryl was entirely too "uppity" for her own good and deserved any and all recriminations she received from us. As we grew older and Cheryl began to date, she was always late, and while her date was waiting in the living room, I flirted with him. Can you imagine how embarrassed Cheryl must have been? Her five-year-old sister was blatantly trying to make a move on her date? I must have thought I was Shirley Temple or something. Then, when Cheryl and her date came home, Annie and Erin would hide under the front porch so they could see them kiss goodnight, and then jump out yelling, "Surprise!"

Annie and Erin played another trick on Cheryl which endeared them to me. They hid in the back seat of the car when some boy came to pick Cheryl up for a date. The whole reason was that Cheryl was so excited because this guy was supposed to be like the most popular guy in school, and he had finally asked her out. She had been planning all week for this one night, and Annie and Erin couldn't resist the temptation to ruin it for her

When Cheryl and her date, Robert, pulled into the dance in Big Lake, Cheryl caught a glimpse of Annie and Erin in the back seat. Then, of course, Robert and Cheryl had to bring them home. Cheryl always looked in the back seat from then on, and Annie was again cleaning windows and sweeping. It's no wonder she hates housework to this day. Maybe Mother felt a little guilty about the fact that Annie and I tormented Cheryl and her friends, so she gave her a big "Sweet Sixteen" party. Cheryl was always popular, so a lot of people came.

I still remember that Mother made a chocolate cake with white icing and blue and yellow decorations with "Sweet Sixteen" written on it. Mother and Daddy let Cheryl play all of her favorite records as loud as she wanted and didn't make anyone leave until midnight. I was always wishing that someday someone would give me a "Sweet Sixteen" party.

That summer was like magic to Cheryl. The swimming

pool in Texon was at the top of a mountain, which could only be reached by driving up a steep and winding, dirt road. The road was so narrow that it would accommodate only one car at a time. If you passed another car, one of the cars had to stop and move over. The rule was, if you were coming down the hill, you stopped for any cars going *up* the hill. Most people were scared that their cars would never make it to the top if they were forced to temporarily pull over.

That following winter one of Cheryl's friends got drunk with a bunch of his buddies and drove up to the pool. I guess they were so drunk they thought it was summer. One of the boys jumped off the high diving board into the empty concrete pool. Of course, he was unconscious and bloody, maybe dead. That sobered the other boys enough that two of them came racing back down into Texon, yelling at the top of their lungs, "Bobby's hurt! We need help fast!"

Cheryl and her date were sitting in the park and ran over to our house. Cheryl bounded in the front door yelling, "Daddy, call an ambulance quick! Bobby got hurt up at the pool, really bad!" Mother called the ambulance in Big Lake, and Daddy jumped in the car and drove as fast as he could up to the pool.

Daddy walked down the pool ladder to help. But, he saw Bobby was dead. He sat there with him until the ambulance arrived. The other boys had already told Bobby's parents about the accident, and when they got up there, Daddy had to tell them Bobby was gone. All I remember is a funeral about two days later in Big Lake. From that time on, they kept the fence around the pool padlocked all winter.

☆ ☆ ☆ ☆ ☆ ☆ ☆ ☆ ☆

I was feeling even more left out of the picture because

Annie stopped giving me so much trouble. I liked the attention even when it was in the form of a prank. But, what I did next got me into more trouble than Annie had ever been in, and I will never forget the *"paint fiasco."* Ever since that day, I have never been fond of the color yellow.

The day started out like any other summer afternoon. The only good thing to come of it was that the other kids no longer called me "Goody-Two Shoes."

"Marcie, I talked to Benjamin Ward's mother today. I told her you would be happy to take him to Susan's birthday party, and he will be here in about twenty minutes, so you had better get ready."

"But, Mommy, Benjamin's just four years old. I can't take him with me. It'll make me look like a baby, too."

"No fussing, Marcie. It'll be just fine. I expect you to introduce him around because he's new and kind of nervous."

My mother would live to regret those words! Not only would I "introduce him around," I'd make him *famous*! Susan's party was a boring, baby party with a clown. BIG DEAL! Anybody who was anybody knew that the only popular shows were Romper Room, Captain Kangaroo, Roy Rogers and Dale Evans. Peter Pan had kind of dimmed as a hero, at least in my mind. There wasn't one clown in that group, so I was not the least impressed.

The only good thing about the party was that Mother let me wear my new white dress from Sears. I only got two new dresses a year—one for Easter and one for the first day of school, and they were always from Sears. The reason I never got anything new was that I had enough older sisters and cousins who always gave me hand-me-downs. Aunt May was a terrific seamstress, so the dresses she sent were always pretty, not like Mother's.

Mother let me wear my new white dress to the party on

the Saturday after Easter, so I had not worn it but one time. I thought it was the prettiest dress ever made. The collar and the short sleeves had light pink lace trim, and Mother had bought me white socks, and gloves with pink lace trim. I also had a pair of white patent leather shoes, and a white straw hat with pink flowers in it. I thought that I was the *epitome* of a Texon fashion plate.

After I was dressed, my mother informed me, "This is your new dress. I don't want you to get anything on it, including dirt and cake. You have to be careful. It's your only church dress."

Benjamin came over in a white pair of shorts with a white shirt and white matching jacket. He would have been kind of cute, but he had orange hair—you know—not red, orange! Apparently his mother also let him wear his Easter clothes to the party. Not only did I have to go to this dull party, but I had to responsibility of taking someone with me. At that exact moment, I knew why Annie hated it when I tagged along.

Our mothers lectured to us before we left for the party to "Absolutely not come back with food on our clothes or even worse, grass stains!" Now, you tell me, don't you think that sounds like too much to hope for from a five-year-old? Especially ones going to a birthday party in the middle of the afternoon? Mother told me that I was to "take care" of Benjamin. Already I was being given adult responsibilities, and I was only five! I do have to admit, however, that I felt bossy and old enough to make Benjamin cringe. He followed me around like a puppy dog.

We got back to my house early, and Mother wasn't there, so, we decided to entertain ourselves. I was feeling sort of cocky and I almost told Benjamin that if he climbed up on the roof of the barn and jumped off, that he would feel like

Peter Pan. I decided that Benjamin wasn't as gullible as I; besides, as we are all aware, that had already been done. In Annie's style, I had to come up with something new and something clever.

We were playing on the new red swing set that Santa had given me that year, when I spotted an open can of bright yellow paint. The possibilities that can of paint produced were endless!

I suggested to Benjamin, "See that can of paint? We should see if we can find some old brushes and paint the house." He agreed and we began painting the side of our white house with a gentle but cheery motif of yellow!

After painting the part of the house that we could reach, we went in search of other possibilities. The swing set! I had never wanted a red swing set anyway, but Mother told me that red was all Santa had. It seemed odd that Santa would run out of the right color of toys so frequently.

Anyway, in the most adult manner I could muster, I told Benjamin, "We should paint the red swing set. I'm kind of mad at Santa Claus anyway. I asked Santa for a yellow swing set anyway. Want to?" Of course, Benjamin agreed. The only problem was that we could only paint the bottom half. If we had found a ladder, we could have performed endless wonders of beauty. As it was now, the bottom half of the swing set was yellow, and the top half was still red.

Since we still had a little yellow paint, I decided to get my doll (also a gift from Santa). She was wearing a pale blue dress with little red flowers. I had named her Patty (after Patty Paige), and we decided since she had blonde hair, that she would look better in a yellow dress. The entire time we were busy improving our surroundings, we were, of course, getting the yellow paint all over our new clothes.

When Mother returned and opened the back door and

saw what we had done, her scream will live forever in Texon infamy, "OH, MY GOD! OH MY GOD! MARCIE LYNN FITZGERALD, GET INTO THE HOUSE RIGHT NOW! OH MY GOD! You stay in the house on the kitchen floor and DO NOT MOVE FROM THAT SPOT UNTIL I GET BACK! DO YOU UNDERSTAND?" "Yes ma'am," I was already starting to cry.

My mother took Benjamin home. I don't know what kind of punishment he received. I just know his mother never let him come over to my house to play again.

When Mother got home, she completely stripped me, put me in the bathtub, and told me to sit there and think about what I had done. I'll never forget it. To make things even worse, *Mother* made me a new dress to replace the one with paint on it. Of course, it looked awful, but I had to wear it and I never did get new white shoes. I had to wear yellow splattered patent leather shoes to church until I *outgrew* them. Mother used white shoe polish on them and they still looked awful. Since I was the only girl my age in Texon, I told the boys that it was a new style.

My mother did not approve of my quest for new adventure, because every time I wore those shoes, she would just shake her head and mutter something hard to understand. I still don't think my painting episode was as bad as Annie's pool hall caper. I would have gladly swept the store instead of wearing a dress Mother had made. I liked to sweep because I had this weird neat thing about me.

☆ ☆ ☆ ☆ ☆ ☆ ☆ ☆ ☆

That summer was like every other summer that I could remember in Texon. Everybody in camp would go to the park on Saturday nights for a picnic. Each family would bring a dish. At least two families always brought ice cream mixers, and we'd make homemade ice cream. We'd eat watermelon and gorge ourselves on sodas. I just loved those nights. I know I will never forget them. It's too bad that tradition is gone because of the fear of violence.

Every Easter, a bunch of the mothers would get together with the kids, and we'd make Easter eggs. Then the mothers would hide the eggs, and after church, we'd get to hunt for them. All the eggs were pretty, but only one egg had a *quarter* taped to it. I never did find the one with the quarter and it kind of tarnished the egg hunt for me, but I still had fun. We all did.

Five

That September, I started the first grade. My birthday is September 18th, so technically I was only five. Texon was just big enough to have two grades, taught by one teacher in the same room. Her name was Mrs. Miller. Can you possibly imagine the patience that woman must have had? Mother Theresa couldn't have done better.

It was in the first grade that I came into my own personality—a total geek with ugly glasses. In those days, a nurse would go to all the schools and hold up a cardboard reading card. If you couldn't read past a certain line, you were told you needed glasses. Well I couldn't, so I had to start the first grade with these glasses my mother bought me. They were the absolute *ugliest* glasses ever worn by a human being. They were yellow (I was no longer too fond of that color), pointed up on the ends to a perfect triangle, and too big for me, so they were always crooked. Much later, about the fourth grade, I finally got smart. They still sent a nurse around with the cardboard letters, but I *memorized* the letters of the people who went in front of me. I was really lucky that they didn't need glasses.

The fact that I was a total *geek* did not banish me from having a boyfriend. The odds were in my favor. I was the only girl in both the first and second grade classes, so I had an edge on the market. Boys were buying me cokes in the afternoon, and Mother even let me walk down to the drug store with a boy for ice cream if I wouldn't be gone too long.

The problem about being the only girl in class carried a lot of social responsibility. I couldn't pay any more attention to one boy than the other. Let me tell you, I was spread pretty thin.

There was one boy that I particularly favored, and I can't even remember his name now. I do remember that one day we picked a spot between the bed sheets hanging on the line across the street from our apartment. We decided this was the perfect place for privacy, and that's where we had our first kiss. I was so excited! I guess we didn't take into account there were some angles by which we were easily seen, like from the front porch of our house. Annie saw us and teased me forever.

"My big brother told me there is no Santa Claus," my no-name first kiss guy told me. "It's just your parents sneaking around in the middle of the night and putting toys under the tree and eating cookies and drinking milk," he informed me in the most solemn manner a first grader could muster.

"I don't believe you," I told him. "Santa Claus always brings me stuff, and how could my parents go and buy all those presents and hide them? I hate you. You're mean. I hope Santa Claus doesn't bring you anything this year." I was pretty receptive to the idea that there really wasn't a Santa Claus; however, in my role as the only girl in two classes, I felt socially compelled to argue for Santa Claus. There was no reason to ruin everyone's Christmas.

Actually, I think I was almost the last person in the first grade to know the truth. I came home upset, and as fate would have it, Annie was at home, too. I told her I had found out that there was no Santa Claus. Annie, always the pragmatic one, confirmed it. Annie said that although there wasn't a Santa Claus, it was better for me to pretend there was, so our parents would feel obligated to fill my list as much as possible. That made a lot of sense to me, but I still wasn't sure. Annie made me look at the handwriting on the notes Santa left me, and sure enough, it was my mother's!

I was mad at my parents for not getting me a yellow swing set instead of a red one, but I didn't say anything about it. I was still in trouble over the paint fiasco. Annie also tried to explain the *Easter Bunny* and *Tooth Fairy*, but I wouldn't hear of it. I had received enough truth for one day. Besides that, I was at the point where a lot of my teeth were falling out. I wasn't about to destroy the *Tooth Fairy* image at that crucial moment.

I think Annie did something that year also, just in order to solidify her role as head troublemaker. She and Erin were in the school band in Big Lake. Annie played the trombone, horribly I might add. There were five chairs of trombone players, and she was fifth. Erin didn't do much better; she played the clarinet. The only thing worse than listening to the *hump, hump, hump* of a bad trombone player was listening to a squeaky clarinet. She played the clarinet and was fourth chair when there were only five chairs.

One night the entire family went to a football game, and there was Annie and Erin marching at half time with the band. Before marching out, they had each sneaked on a big nose and glasses like you find in specialty stores and marched onto the field with the other band members.

Several things occurred. My mother read Annie *the riot act* for about the one thousandth time. The band leader was mad, but powerless. How could he demote them? They were so far down the line anyway. They both got a "C" in band. My father was perturbed about the "C." He sat Annie down and told her that he never expected to see another bad grade on her report card again, especially since he knew she could do better. She was back to sweeping the store floors for a month.

I was in the second grade when I had a another bad experience. I was waiting for Annie to come to the school and take me over to Aunt Bessie's, because that was where my mother was. I sat in front of the school as I had been instructed to do by my mother. The only problem was that I picked an ant bed to sit on. By the time Annie picked me up, I was covered in ant bites and screaming and crying. You would think I would have gotten the message that my choice of sitting spots was not a very good idea, wouldn't you? Not me though. I just sat there and patiently waited for Annie. And got bitten about fifty or sixty times. The entire time my mother was putting salve on the bites, she said, "Why didn't you just move?" I don't know why I didn't. I guess I was just as stubborn as the rest of the family.

The first day of second grade got me into trouble. Tommy's mother, Mrs. Miller, and my parents were all mad at me. When my mother came to pick me up at school, Mrs. Miller told her that I had kicked Tommy in the nose and made it bleed. My mother was upset. Mrs. Miller asked, "Why on earth did you kick Tommy in the nose, Marcie? That's not like you."

"Because he kept dropping his pencil on purpose so he could look up my skirt." If I hadn't kicked Tommy in the nose, he probably would have gone clear through school dropping his pens and pencils and looking up girls' skirts. I personally think I did him a favor. I think Mrs. Miller and Mother were too busy holding back their laughs to punish me.

Trying to retrieve my homework also got me in trouble. It wasn't my fault. I was doing my math homework on the kitchen table, and Cheryl put the paper in the trash can when she cleaned up the kitchen. For once in Cheryl's life as a teenager, she decided to be neat, and threw my homework away.

I *had* to find my homework; I wasn't about to do it all over again. I hate math! I went outside and stuck my hand in the big tin garbage can and was promptly stung by a scorpion. You could have heard my screaming for miles. The next day in school, when my right hand was all red and swollen, I told Mrs. Miller the truth, and she didn't make me do it over. In fact, because I am right-handed, she even let me get off from doing my homework for the rest of the week. If the scorpion bite hadn't hurt so much, it would have been worth using that excuse forever. It was a lot better excuse than, "My dog ate it," something Annie might use.

Christmas that year was another time when my mother embarrassed me. We had a combination Christmas party (first and second grade). We had put up a tree and was making decorations for a month. Since I was the only girl, I got to do a lot of the decorating, and I was proud of my artistic ability. Each decoration that we made individually we got to take home. We exchanged names and bought presents for the person whose name we drew, and we were allowed to spend fifty cents on each gift. The mothers were asked to come help with the party.

While we were opening our gifts, my mother backed into the tree. It all came tumbling down, lights and everything. I was embarrassed and cried for hours. Mrs. Miller tried to make me take some of the decorations home, but I was too humiliated. Also, most of them were broken. Who wants smashed ornaments?

That same year, Santa Claus brought Annie a neat present. I remember waking up about four in the morning and running and jumping on Annie's bed. I was yelling, "Wake up, Annie! Santa brought you a BB gun!" We had the whole house up by that time. Annie had been asking for a BB gun for a whole year but was certain she wouldn't get it. She took it over to Erin's house for target practice, and the first thing she did was to kill a sparrow. She came home in tears, "I hate that gun." She put the BB gun away and never used it again. That was one of the very few times I had ever seen Annie cry. The eyelash affair almost did it, but not quite. At least the BB gun was one weapon she didn't use on me.

That Christmas was also the first time that Mother and Daddy waited until Christmas Eve to decorate the tree. I remember pestering my Mother at least once a day for a month about decorating because everyone else I knew already had their tree up. Instead of buying a tree in Big Lake, we girls went out with Daddy on Christmas Eve to find a tree to chop down while Mother was in the store. That night we started making decorations. We strung popcorn, colored paper figures, hung up painted ornaments, had non-alcohol eggnog, sang Christmas carols, and hung up the lights from the year before. We had a great time! I thought it was the best Christmas I ever had.

I wonder how much was due to the fact that we didn't have the money to make Christmas ornaments or to buy a tree? But, but that's okay, because we all had a terrific time. The cost of that stupid BB gun though, probably had something to do with it. I guess Annie really did learn a lesson from it. And there really is something special when you wait until Christmas Eve to decorate the tree. We were so busy decorating that we never even once pestered my parents about opening any presents that night.

Another problem presented itself in the second grade. I was a big fan of *Romper Room*. Santa brought me a stick horse for Christmas. I wanted to stay home and watch *Romper Room* on television instead of going to school because they were going to have someone special on that day. I pretended to be sick, so Mother let me stay home. The only problem was, when she came into the apartment I was riding my stick horse and singing with the *Romper Room* crowd like crazy! She promptly made me get dressed and go to school with an apology to Mrs. Miller. Santa Claus always got me into trouble.

I guess since the BB gun was such a desperate failure they decided to buy a piano. It was a present for all of us and I guess they felt that it was far better for us to learn something more constructive than shooting guns and jumping off barns.

Six

My parents had to save for quite a long time to buy that piano, but they finally were able to afford one when I was still in second grade. They tried without success to convince my older sisters to take piano lessons. Cheryl flatly refused. Annie took lessons for about three or four months and then gave it up. She just wasn't interested. Rather than waste an expensive budget-crunching instrument, they had Mrs. Collins give me lessons. Guess what? I loved it. I really did and didn't mind practicing at all.

My love for the piano must have been tied in somehow

with that compulsive perfectionist stuff I was experiencing. For one thing, Mrs. Collins never learned how to keep time. She was also hard of hearing. She could make out the melody okay and teach me the notes, but couldn't do too much for the timing. I personally think Mrs. Collins had a few bats loose in her belfry, even though she was nice to me.

I played the notes perfectly, but I pretty much made up the rhythm. Have you ever heard "Silent Night" played to the rhythm of the title song from "Gunsmoke?" It might not have always sounded "just right," but at least I tried. It helped me with my self-confidence. I was finally able to do something that Cheryl and Annie couldn't!

I got away with not knowing about timing. Since Texon wasn't exactly the piano Capitol of the world, making up my own rhythm was a lot more interesting than all that counting business. My father was content to have at least one of us show some interest in music, since that was something he enjoyed.

My success with the piano earned me a spot on a children's show in Midland. I had hit the BIG TIME! A princess appeared in a beautiful gown and sang and played games. You could send your name and a drawing was held every week. If your name was drawn, you could have your birthday party on TV, and you could invite five of your friends to come along. Well, one of my friends, Gary, had his name called. Gary's mother not only invited me but also called the television station and arranged for me to play a song on the air. I thought it would be great and imagined that I would become an overnight musical sensation.

Gary's mother drove us to Midland, and we bet on the color of the princess' dress on the way, since colored television didn't even exist in 1956. I won the bet. Her dress was pink, but I was disappointed with her magic wand. It was just the round cardboard from the center of a coat hangar that had glitter glued all over it. I think she was also wearing a wig because I noticed it slip a couple of times.

My song sounded okay, I guess. What happened after that was so traumatic that it probably ruined my burgeoning career as a concert pianist. I had a sudden bout of stage fright! Each kid waved at the TV camera, said their name, and waved goodbye, just like the *Mouseketeers.*

When the camera was pointed at me, all I could do was stand there with my mouth open. I felt like falling in a hole and never coming out. No one but my parents remembered that I had just performed a musical feat comparable to Mozart; the only thing all the other kids remembered was that I stood there like I was frozen stiff with my mouth agape and unable to speak a single word. I *forgot* my name!

I was teased unmercifully by all the other kids in Texon, but Annie didn't tease me. My mother probably talked to her before we got back home. I cried for days because I was so embarrassed and vowed never to go on television again. Not for one second did I think that it really didn't matter because I would never be asked to be on television anyway. My friend, Benjamin, tried to console me by saying that maybe he couldn't have said his name either. That didn't help. After all, he was a year younger than me; he was a baby.

My grandfather believed that I played like Mozart. When we went to the nursing home where he was living, he always had me play the piano for his friends. They clapped like they were hearing an orchestra. I suppose my Grandfather was just happy that we loved him enough to visit him, but I believe he was also proud of me.

Before Grandpa went to the nursing home to live, he would come visit us and always had candy or gum in his pockets to give out to the kids. He liked to talk to everyone. It never dawned on me that the candy and gum probably came from our store. He was a great storyteller, and I remember how much the kids liked him. They would follow him around and fight over who got to sit in his lap. He remembered nearly everyone's name. I was proud of him. I thought he was the most wonderful grandfather in the world.

Grandpa was 96 years old when he got the German measles. We didn't have vaccinations for the measles then, and they made him quite sick. I remember visiting him again when he was better, and he was complaining about the old man in the bed next to his. That man was 78. It never occurred to him that he was eighteen years older than that "old" man. Grandpa died when he was 98. Good memories are all I carried in my heart for Grandpa.

☆ ☆ ☆ ☆ ☆ ☆ ☆ ☆ ☆

After my mild success on TV and in the nursing home, I still managed to embarrass my mother that year. Sometimes I think that's what children do best. It was when our minister called. He recognized my voice and wished me a happy birthday. I said "thank you" but I didn't recognize his voice and he neglected to say who it was.

Anyway, my mother wasn't feeling very well that day, and she was in the bathroom. Then he asked to speak to my mother. I told him she couldn't come to the phone right this minute because she was on the toilet and that she had a serious case of diarrhea! I think he secretly laughed about it. Kids, in their innocence, oftentimes say the goofiest things. When he identified himself I quickly hung up the phone.

Mother heard the phone ring and asked who called. I told her it was the minister and that he wished me a "Happy Birthday." I thought I had been rather cool. You just never can tell about adults and I didn't lie, I just didn't tell her *all* the truth. Grownups get upset over the slightest things.

☆ ☆ ☆ ☆ ☆ ☆ ☆ ☆ ☆

Texon had sufficient population to warrant forming a nondenominational church, which we attended every Sunday morning and evening and on Wednesday night, something all devout Baptists do. I suppose the minister pretty much stayed in line with the Baptist teachings, or my mother would have insisted we go somewhere else. Now that I think about it, Mother should have become a Baptist minister and I should have been Japanese.

My mother would have been absolutely *mortified* had she known that when I was just seven years old, my friend David and I would sit in one of the back pews of the church and play poker or gin rummy. Which game we chose always depended on how long we thought the sermon would last. Our church was not large enough to support its own minister, so we depended on traveling ministers for Sundays. If the ministers were Presbyterian or Lutheran, we usually chose to play poker because we assumed the sermon wouldn't last long. If the ministers were Baptist, we *knew* we were in there for the long stretch. Those days were good gin rummy days.

I can only hope that the points I earned with God for my cleanliness streak overcame the sin of playing cards in church. David and I would mime the words so that everyone in church would think we were singing. Come to think of it, my voice is so awful, I think David suggested it. Whatever, it worked, and church was where I actually perfected my skill at card playing. My parents would have skinned me alive had they caught me.

Only about half of the usual congregation showed up

on Wednesday night, but my family was *always* there. My mother's philosophy about church attendance was that, "We could skip church only if we were in the hospital or dead." On Wednesday night, the adults in the audience took turns delivering the sermons. That was the ultimate boring time.

Usually someone just stood at the pulpit and read from the Bible. Most of the adults had absolutely no experience in public speaking and read scripture as if they were on high doses of Valium. Yes, Wednesday nights were definitely gin rummy nights. I have no idea why Annie or Cheryl didn't tell my parents what we were doing, unless they were afraid I would squeal on them for sneaking out of the house from time to time.

Cheryl and Annie had been sneaking out of the house for about two years. I know because we all slept in the same bedroom. They both bribed me so many times with promises to buy me chocolate milkshakes that if I wanted to, I could have been the fattest kid in Texas. I knew better than to tell. Annie would have sought revenge.

My piano skills were good enough by Texon standards for me to play in church. It really wasn't that I was a musical prodigy; I just liked it well enough and practiced enough so that I could fill in for the normal piano lady. Sometimes the church even had me play special songs. Boy, did I think I was important! They undoubtedly had me play in order to relieve some of the boredom that existed during the regular Wednesday night Bible reading when they read to each other.

On Sundays, the traveling ministers were usually so excited about their mission of bringing religion to our "isolated region," that they really worked themselves into a sort of frenzy. I personally think they were mostly frustrated missionaries who never made it to the far corners of the earth, and they released all that religious fervor upon us. I am certain that most of them were disappointed to discover that we could read and speak their language and didn't live in huts.

They would rant and rave about fire and brimstone so much that it scared me and sometimes I had nightmares. I just knew I was on the *bad list* and would burn in eternal damnation. That must have been the 1950's version of violence on television.

There were times that their sermons "reached me" and I would go up to the front to be "saved." I hoped God would forget I had been up there to be "saved" the week before. After doing that about five times, my Mother grabbed me by the collar of my dress, "Marcie, you don't have to go up there. God knows you're saved, so please just sit." I knew I was saved, but I couldn't stop going up to the front. I had decided for a while that maybe I could be a missionary in Africa or some other forsaken part of the world. It didn't take me long to forget that notion. As glamourous as that sounded, I discarded the idea as soon as I reasoned that the parts of the world which were in need of spiritual and economic guidance usually came with giant spiders, ants, snakes, bugs and no exterminators. I've always hated bugs.

☆ ☆ ☆ ☆ ☆ ☆ ☆ ☆ ☆

When I was almost seven, my mother let me spend the night with Marie. I was so excited because it was my first time to spend the night with a friend. She lived down the street, but you would think I was going on a mission to the moon by the way I packed. I was wondering why she invited me, because Marie didn't seem to like me very much. Maybe her mother made her ask me, but I didn't care.

That night we had a snowstorm. That's rare in West Texas, but sometimes it will snow about four or five inches.

Because of the storm, my father came down to Marie's house to pick me up. As he was buttoning up my coat, I looked outside the front windows and said, "Boy, it sure is snowing to beat hell out there."

I got into so much trouble over that one little phrase. I don't think God was really mad at me for that, since it was the truth. Besides, those ministers said "hell" just about every other word. And it's in the Bible! If you aren't supposed to say words that are in the Bible, then what words are you supposed to say? I guess "hell" isn't one of them.

Marie's big sister was a girl named Henrietta, "Etta" for short. She had the brightest red hair I had ever seen, big green eyes, was a very tall 5' 11", and Cheryl's best friend. Etta told Cheryl that her parents laughed for days about what I had said about the snowstorm. At least there were some people who appreciated it. It was so funny to see Etta and Cheryl together. They looked like Mutt and Jeff because Cheryl was only 5' 2".

To make certain that I had not offended God in any way, I volunteered my services as piano player more often. You know, to even up the score. I guess my mother didn't agree with my rationalization why "hell" wasn't a curse word. She was probably shaking her head, thinking, "I've got another Annie on my hands!"

My concept of how each person was chosen to go to heaven was that God was sitting in heaven with a tally sheet. One side was the "Good" side and the other side read "Bad." Whenever you committed a sin, God would place a mark under "Bad," and if you did something nice, He would make His mark under "Good." Then He would add up the marks on the tally sheet when you died, and if the Good had more marks than the Bad, you got in through the gates of heaven. If the total added up more marks under Bad, you went to Hell.

Since no one *knows* what really happens until after death, there isn't any proof, so I guess it's pretty much "call 'em as you see 'em." I thought if you were a minister or a missionary, God probably gave you about ten extra marks for good behavior.

God must have been a busy guy. I had a good idea how my tally sheet was going. I know I got bad marks whenever I played cards in Church, but I was young and had a lot of time to make up for it. Besides, when I played the piano in Church, I probably made a couple of good points. God would probably overlook the card playing and cursing if I "saved" myself a lot and promised to become a better person when I grew up. Now I had to find out exactly what it was that God wanted me to do to make up for all the bad marks. I could become a piano teacher, but Mrs. Collins hadn't taught me how to keep time, so I ruled that out. Otherwise, we'd have a whole lot more people playing the piano who couldn't keep time.

I had systematically ruled out appearing on television, singing, playing the piano, and being a missionary as career choices, and I was only seven years old. But there was plenty of time to find out. I hoped I inherited some of my family's better qualities and not all of its weird ones, like my Grandmother Molly. Not that Grandma didn't have good qualities, she was just so weird, it was sometimes impossible to see them.

☆ ☆ ☆ ☆ ☆ ☆ ☆ ☆ ☆

This grandmother, Molly, was my mother's mother. She was the widow of two Baptist ministers. She was also as crazy as a bedbug. Even my mother had to admit that. She must have come from pioneering stock. Grandma chewed snuff and spit it out in a coffee can. When she came to visit us, that habit would drive my mother bonkers, but no matter how much Mother begged her to stop, she wouldn't. I can say this much for her, she could hold her own with any baseball player. One thing in her favor is that she never scratched. She was stubborn as a mule. As far as I know, she chewed snuff until the day she died and never missed the can to spit.

I think Grandma was born in the wrong age. She never understood television. When "I Love Lucy" came on the air, she would set up her TV stand in the living room and "have dinner" with the Ricardos. She honestly believed that Lucy, Desi, and Little Rickie were having dinner with her and visiting in her living room. She was so thrilled when little Rickie was born that she called my mother to make sure she had heard the news.

Grandma didn't want us to miss it. She thought that maybe the whole family could combine the money to buy Lucy a nice present for little Rickie. I don't remember how Mother convinced her that it wasn't necessary to send presents. I can remember incessant explanations by my mother in which she tried to explain what television really was. It never did any good, so my mother just gave up.

I remember visiting Grandma when I was about seven. We girls were walking in Grandma's living room while "the Ricardos were visiting." My grandma had an absolute fit because we were wearing our pajamas in front of company.

She yelled from across the room, "You girls go back in that bedroom right this minute and change into some decent clothes. Is this the way your mother taught you to behave around company?"

Cheryl, being the oldest and therefore the most worldly replied, "Grandma, it's just television. It's all on some sort of tape. We can see them, but they can't see us." Cheryl was thoroughly convinced at this point that she had explained the idea sufficiently to Grandma. She obviously hadn't.

"If you three girls *do not* go back into that room and change instantly, I will spank you myself! Rickie and Lucy will be leaving soon, and then you can come back in here wearing your pajamas!" That was the end of the conversation.

Grandma also lived in constant fear of . . . THE RUSSIANS! I remember once that she called us in order to warn us that THE RUSSIANS were invading the country and to "take cover," whatever that meant. She called when we were eating dinner. My mother tried to calm her down, but she just couldn't. Actually, Grandma was watching a movie about Roman soldiers. The movie had chariots and persecuted Christians in it, you know, the whole nine yards. Grandma actually believed that THE RUSSIANS had invaded the United States in chariots, and that they were going to persecute us for being Baptist by throwing us to the lions. Mother had to call the relative who lived nearest to Grandma to go over to her house and calm her down. THE RUSSIANS represented a great threat to my grandmother.

I was about six when Grandma came on the bus to visit us in Texon. Besides being absolutely crazy, she was also very hard of hearing. I remember that I was in the apartment in the back of the store and somehow got myself locked in a closet.

For about two hours I screamed, "GRANDMA! GRANDMA! HELP! I'M IN THE CLOSET! HELP!" She never heard me. I guess she never wondered where I was either. Maybe she thought THE RUSSIANS had kidnapped me.

Grandma's house didn't have any warmth except for an electric heater in the living room. When I was seven, Grandma accidentally walked too close to it and caught her dress on fire. She had the presence of mind to run outside and roll around in the grass, so her burns were minimal. The only problem was that she had a tall front porch, so she broke her hip in the process. I went to Comanche with Mother on the bus so that we could take care of Grandma when she got home from the hospital. At first I was really excited about getting out of school for two weeks, but do you know how impossible it is for a seven-year-old to converse with a person who thinks the Roman Army is actually the Russian Army? I thought maybe by turning on the television, we wouldn't have to talk to each other, but when she saw that Rickie and Lucy were seeing her in bed, she *really* got upset. Mother made me promise not to turn on the television in front of Grandma ever again. I didn't.

I hope that I don't ever inherit whatever it was that made Grandma so weird. My Grandmother was set in her ways, and she probably wouldn't have changed even if she could have. A stubborn streak seems to run in our family.

Our mother died of cancer when I was fourteen, and Grandmother was in a nursing home by that time. Grandma never did understand that Mother had died earlier that year, which is probably just as well. Annie looked so much like my mother that when we went to visit her, Annie would pretend to be my mother so that Grandma could talk to her. It must have been difficult for Annie, but she never complained. I think it was one of the kindest things I have ever seen anyone do. I know that it comforted my grandmother in her later years to think that Mother was by her side. I think that Annie made a lot of points with God on her "Good" side. I know she made a lot of points with me.

Seven

Grandma was not the only one entranced by television in the 1950's. Everyone was amazed by it and didn't know anything about it. Similar to the way most people viewed computers about ten years ago. Do you remember the show where Dinah Shore sang and then kissed everyone goodbye? That show was my fourth favorite. My order of preference was Romper Room, Captain Kangaroo, the show with the Princess (that love kind of floundered after my dismal debut), and then the Dinah Shore show. I always wanted to look like Dinah Shore or Patty Paige when I grew up. I thought my friend Marie was just as pretty and as sophisticated as either one.

Marie Stone was a girl one year older than I, whom I spent the night with when I had gotten into so much trouble for saying "hell." She had beautiful, long, thick auburn hair, and considered herself much more sophisticated than I. She was stuck-up, but I never stopped idolizing her. I pestered her at least once a day. Besides the fact that I thought Marie was the most glamourous person in Texon, she was the closest girl to my age. My favorite thing was to play with Patty Page paper dolls, and Marie's favorite pastime was to play cards. We always played cards at her house though and not at mine. Being the good Baptist that she was, Mother didn't forbid me to play cards but certainly didn't encourage it.

Marie would sometimes tell her mother to say that she was somewhere else when I came over, just so I would leave her alone, but I always knew she was home. Where else would she be? Texon was *really* small. Besides, I was a big pest. It never made a difference to me that she didn't always want to play with me. I liked Marie nevertheless. I think every girl remembers the one other girl who always made the best grades, had the neatest boyfriends, and always found the Easter Egg with the quarter taped to it. That was Marie. I think it is a burden God must have put upon all the rest of us mere mortals, just to keep us humble. I also thought Marie was as pretty as Dinah Shore and courageous as Dale Evans.

I did have one redeeming quality in which Marie never did manage to excel. My talent as the "Hula Hoop Queen" of Texon was never matched by anyone. I could hula hoop longer than any other girl in Texon. Once I discovered my natural ability, I hula hooped everywhere. Mother put a stop to hula hooping in the house though. I guess she imagined all kinds of broken things left in my path. It's a good thing I was good at hula hooping because I was always clumsy in every other sport. Do you know what it's like always being the last one picked for sides? "Okay, I'll take Marcie since she's the only one left." Well, thanks a lot. There aren't any sides in hula hooping. Just think—if there had been a hula hoop team, I might have been a hula hoop professional or an Olympic champion.

Of course, I also beat Marie with the dimple thing, too. "Aunt Bessie," my mother's friend always favored me. I think she liked me regardless of my dimples and hula hoop ability. Anytime I went over she would offer me cookies, cake, biscuits, or anything else that was in her kitchen. It was like suddenly discovering a new restaurant down the street. The only problem was that she had a little Pekinese dog that was the meanest dog on the face of the earth. I bet those lions Grandma was so afraid of would even have been scared of that little dog. Aunt Bessie would have to come outside and chain her dog before anyone was allowed inside her gate. That dog bit me once, and that was all it took for me to wait for Aunt Bessie to calm her down before going into her house.

My mother and Aunt Bessie were good friends. One

day when I was about seven, someone in Texon died, and his funeral was in Big Lake. I don't even remember who died, but Mother said when she asked Aunt Bessie if she wanted a ride to the funeral, she said, "No. He won't be coming to mine." Aunt Bessie always told it like it was. Even though Mother thought that wasn't very religious of her, she still thought it was funny. She and Aunt Bessie became inseparable friends.

One of Cheryl's friends in Texon was a girl named Cindy. I think Cindy liked to hang around Cheryl because she was so popular. Maybe she thought if she hung around long enough, some of the popularity would rub off. Cindy was a little chubby. She had brown hair, brown eyes, weighed about 160 pounds and wasn't very tall, but she never forgot any of our birthdays. She always came over with a big box of chocolate-covered cherries. The only thing is, Cindy knew that none of us liked cherries, so she got to eat the whole box by herself! I guess it was still nice of her to remember. I have had many "friends" since then whom never remember my birthday.

One time for my birthday Annie tried to bake something for me just to be nice. I couldn't believe it. Not that Annie wasn't nice, I just didn't think she would do it for *me!* My favorite dessert was anything chocolate, so she decided to make brownies. The recipe called for "mixing by hand." Mother came in from the store to see if she could lend Annie some help, and there was Annie—her hand in the mixing bowl with all the ingredients. Annie just couldn't understand why Mother was laughing so hard. After all, it did say "mix by hand." Poor Annie, that just wasn't a good year for her.

My mother was a wonderful cook. She made a pecan pie one Sunday morning and placed it on the window sill to cool while we were in church. The only problem was that someone let the pet canary out of his cage that morning. When we got home from church, the canary was on the window sill beside the pie. He was dead. I guessed he choked on a pecan or something. It was quite a while before Mother made pecan pie again. I didn't like that bird anyway. I think dogs and cats are nicer because they like to be cuddled. Besides, they're smart enough to know that pecans should be chewed before swallowed.

That year, the school in Big Lake where Annie and Cheryl attended formed a girl's basketball team. That was progressive in the 1950's. Annie had never seen anything but a football game. That was before televised sports, of course. Annie's team was ahead during the first basketball game they played, so the coach, Mr. Sanderson, put Annie in the game. Annie got really confused. She picked up that basketball, and with every ounce of energy in her body, ran down to the wrong end of the court. She thought she was making a touchdown and was so proud of herself. Poor Annie. I felt sorry for her that time because I knew how she felt. It is pretty funny when you think about it though. Annie wasn't in a very good mood for a whole week, and then she was back to being "Annie."

I was always the worst athlete in school. The only athletic things I could do, were roller skate, bowl and, of course, hula hoop. Those sports are not taken in school, and let's face it, almost anyone can bowl and roller skate. Hula hoop is different though. I was still a Master Hula Hoop Player, and that title has never been challenged. Mother and Daddy always claimed that everyone has to be good at something. I guess hula hooping, skating, and playing the piano was it for me.

A new family moved into the camp that year also. We rarely had new families, and I never had a girl my own age to play with. The new folks' daughter was Kelly Roberts. I was so excited about having someone new that I began going over there a lot, and Kelly came over to our house, too. Kelly had a younger sister and two older brothers. Kelly's dad built a house for Kelly and her sister made of wood in which they could play. It had a staircase and everything! I was envious.

Mr. Roberts seemed really nice, but Kelly's mother hardly ever came out of the house. One day I asked my mother why she never came out to talk to anyone, and she said she didn't really know but not to ask Kelly too many questions because it might embarrass her. Then about three or four months after the Roberts had moved into the camp, an ambulance came all the way from Big Lake! Mrs. Roberts was really sick. Kelly was crying, and I felt sorry for her. Mother took some food over for Kelly and her sister and brothers and kind of kept an eye on them when their dad was at the hospital with their mom.

Two weeks after Mrs. Roberts had gone to the hospital, they moved. Annie said that Mr. Roberts would get drunk and beat Mrs. Roberts, and she almost died this last time. I couldn't believe it. Mr. Roberts seemed like such a nice man.

Mother overheard the conversation and told us, "Mr. Roberts had been told that if he ever beat any of his family, the oil company would not only fire him but also report him to the police. Annie, I don't want you to mention anything about this to anyone. You either, Marcie. We may not have much, but at least we never hurt anyone. You should feel very lucky just to have a home where you aren't always afraid."

I never found out what happened to Kelly and her family until a few years later. I know I missed her. It was beyond my comprehension how anyone nice enough to make a special little house for his children could be so mean to them, too. As I got older, I finally realized that Mr. Roberts must have been an alcoholic. I wish that I had been nicer to Kelly. She must have needed a close friend.

There were a lot of new changes in my life that year. It was my first time to ride a bus to school and to meet a lot of new people. I would no longer be the only girl in the class, and I would no longer be able to just run home if something happened.

I remember the first time I got on the bus, the bus driver looked at me with mean eyes and snarled, "You're Annie Morgan's little sister, aren't you?"

I meekly replied, "Yes, sir, my name is Marcie Fitzgerald." (My parents told us to always call adults "sir or ma'am," no matter how mean they were).

Besides, part of the driver's cranky disposition with me was Annie's fault. She was constantly in trouble for everything from running up and down the aisles to pitching wads of chewing gum. The bus driver even made Annie get off the bus on the way home one afternoon, about a mile from Texon, and told her that she had to walk the rest of the way. Out of loyalty, Cheryl got off with her. Boy, was my mother mad at that driver! The next morning my mother was waiting for the bus. She told Annie and Cheryl to get in the bus. Then she told the bus driver as calmly as she could, "If you *ever* make any of my children walk home again or make them get off the bus out in the middle of nowhere, you'll have to deal with me and my husband. It's unsafe, and I'll report you to the school district. If my children do something wrong, send me a note. I'll see that they're properly punished."

The driver probably remembered the chewing out my mother gave him; however, being the meek eight-year-old that I was, that bus driver scared me to death, and I tried my hardest to be good so I wouldn't get thrown off the bus. Annie, of course, was not phased in the least by the bus driver. You had to be pretty tough to scare Annie. In fact, you still do.

That year, I also remember having to walk down to

where the bus picked up the oil camp children. Back then, all the girls had to wear dresses to school. Since we lived in West Texas, the dirt and wind combined made huge tumbleweeds. Nothing stings as much as a rolling tumbleweed does on bare legs, except, of course, for a stinging scorpion. Those tumbleweeds seemed to follow you everywhere you went, hunting you down with a vengeance and then attaching themselves to your body like huge, thorny magnets. The dust would blow so hard that by the time we got to school, we were filthy.

Third grade was different in other respects also. We rode the school bus with the black children in the area. I know it's hard to believe, but I had never seen a black person, except on television. Texon was an insulated community. The driver made the black kids sit in the rear of the bus. They even went to an all black school. That was the way it was in Texas in 1958.

One day in the beginning of third grade, I remember two black girls, one about ten, and the other about six, got on the bus. The six-year-old sat in the front row because she didn't know any better. The bus driver turned around and growled, "You and your kind have to sit in the back seats. You don't belong up here in the front." I hoped that God was putting two marks under "Bad" for that bus driver. I remember the little girl crying all the way to school.

I distinctly remember wondering what made that little girl different from me. We were both scared to go to school, both obviously wearing new clothes, but I could sit anywhere on the bus I pleased. I had blonde hair and blue eyes, and Marie had auburn hair and green eyes. No one told us we couldn't sit together. That little black girl's face had a look of pain and embarrassment on it, and the bus driver seemed smug when he told her to move to the back.

Third grade was also my first time to hear the term "white trash." That term was used in reference to all of the oil camp kids. Because we lived in Texon, we were "white trash" with lousy morals and bad manners. It's odd that until the third grade, I felt very special and fortunate just because I *did* live in Texon. I guess that was another thing that made Marie and me more alike — the fact that we must both be "white trash." Then I started wondering if was better to be black than "white trash" or better to be "white trash" than black.

I also wondered how they could think that I didn't have good morals just because I lived in an oil camp. Sure, I played cards in church some of the time, but I still kept up my part of the bargain with God. I probably had already, at age eight, gone to church more than anyone on the bus, with the exception of Annie and Cheryl. My family could also testify to the fact that I had also been *saved* a lot.

I asked my mother why some of the kids called us "white trash." She told me, "Marcie, some people just have to assume that they are better than you. It makes them feel important. Don't worry about it. They'll like you for who you are. If they don't, it's their loss because you and your sisters are wonderful. Maybe they're just jealous. You don't need those people as friends anyway."

Things only got worse when I was faced with about forty new people in the third grade. I think I must have been pretty much a *geek.* You know, one of those people whose picture is beside the word "geek" or "nerd" in the dictionary. That was me. I felt like I never fit in. The other kids were accustomed to having 20 or 30 people in a class, but I wasn't.

The year started very badly for me. Every person in the third grade had to be the hall monitor for a week. The kids could hardly wait to be a monitor because they could let all of their friends off easy for chewing gum, being late, swearing, etc. But not me. Being the nerd that I was and not accustomed to the social status placed upon me, I took being a hall monitor very seriously. Besides, Roy Rogers wouldn't have just let everyone off. Dinah Shore wouldn't have either.

When you became a hall monitor, the teacher gave you a badge to wear and also a pad so you could write down people's names beside their alleged offenses. The first day that I was hall monitor, I wrote down all of the offenses with a vengeance that would have pleased Cagney & Lacey. Only problem was, I forgot to write down the names of the offenders. I was of course, the butt of jokes for the rest of the year. I decided that law enforcement was not in my future either. All I wanted to do was go home.

The only good thing that I can remember about third grade was the Christmas play. Out of all of the third graders, I was picked to be the narrator for the play because I read so well. Mother and Daddy both were proud of me. Aunt Bessie watched the store while they came to the play. I remember that they took a lot of pictures, but I never have been able to find them.

My teacher, Mrs. Willis, sat beside Mother in the audience. Mother said that Mrs. Willis told her, "Marcie is a delight to have in class because she is so well behaved and tries so hard. Marcie is also academically better prepared for the third grade, but then the majority of the Texon students are." She certainly didn't think we were "white trash".

Another thing I remember about the third grade was not so pleasant. Mother started making Annie take me to the drive-in movies in Big Lake when she went with her friends. She gave Annie the money for my ticket and extra for a Coke. Annie, however, had different ideas. She made me get in the trunk of the car right before we got to Big Lake so she wouldn't have to pay for my ticket. She would wait until we were inside the fence to let me get out of the trunk. I just knew I was going to get caught and be put in jail or something. Annie told me that I could have something to eat with the money that Mother gave her for my ticket, but I still don't think that made up for taking a chance at getting caught. I thought maybe they had a jail for kids like me who had just broken the law, and I knew they were going to arrest me and call my parents. I thought maybe "ticket policemen" were hired for that reason. I had a big imagination. Annie told me if I told Mother what we had done, that she would make us all go back to the drive-in and confess to the owners.

Sometimes, though, Annie or Cheryl would take me roller skating or bowling in Big Lake. I liked that because they couldn't sneak me into those places and therefore, I wasn't always on the alert for the ticket police. I remember the first time I went bowling and Cheryl was trying to show me how to bowl and accidentally dropped the bowling ball on my hand. It hurt so much that all I could tearfully say was, "Now you've finally done it! You've ruined my chance of becoming a better bowler."

I was a good roller skater. At least I managed to keep up with Annie and Cheryl enough to harass them. The boys were always trying to skate with Cheryl, so Annie and I finally doubled forces and harassed her. That was fun because I had usually been the victim of Annie's jokes, not her partner. Cheryl was mad at us, but she didn't tell Mother, because then Mother would feel required to give her the same lecture about being careful around boys. As much as Mother talked to Cheryl, it's a wonder she wasn't scared to death of boys!

We went roller skating one Halloween and it was great! They let you in for half-price and gave away candy and gum. Then Cheryl and Annie took me *trick or treating* in Big Lake one Halloween. There were many houses and therefore more people to bother than in Texon. I remember that I went as Casper the Friendly Ghost. He was popular in the comic books at that time. I always read Casper and Little Lulu. I think Annie was like Little Lulu except for the dark hair. When I told her I thought she should dress up like Little Lulu, she got mad at me! She told me in no uncertain terms that costumes like that were for babies like me. I was not a baby—just a young person. That was pretty rude.

Right after the third grade, the oil company that owned Texon sold its property rights to another company and every family there was told to leave. Our family moved to Rankin, and some of the other families moved to Big Lake. It was a profound change for all of us. It meant that our town was no longer like "one big family." Marie and her family moved to Big Lake and Aunt Bessie moved to San Angelo. She had an apartment over her garage and rented it to college students.

When my oldest sister, Cheryl, first attended college, she rented a room from Aunt Bessie. Erin and her family moved to Rankin like we did. Those days in Texon will never return, unfortunately. They remind me of the Norman Rockwell pictures, where things are innocent and people are mindful of others' feelings. I think that's something that we have lost and I will always miss.

The years we spent in Texon remind me of what sociologists are now calling "cocooning." We were like that in a sense because each of us felt that Texon was such a special place that we had no need to look further, and we always knew that if we needed help of any kind, that we would find it there among our friends. I think of Texon as the last place that I ever felt completely safe and totally loved. Texon reminded me of a sort of mystical fairy tale world where you were loved by everyone you met and helped by anyone who came your way. Nothing since then was ever the same.

Eight

"Girls, it is going to be a huge change living here in Rankin. Your mother and I will be working more to make enough money to pay bills and to put aside some money so all of you can go to college. You will do your best not to cause any trouble (all of us automatically looked at Annie). Marcie, you won't be able to run to us any time you need us like you did in the store. We are depending on you all to help us around here, too."

My father wasn't exaggerating. Rankin was so different, and I hated it for years after we moved. For the first few years there, I had only one friend, and I knew very few any of the adults. It was no longer possible for us to just walk around and say hello to everyone the way we did in Texon. Not that we were suddenly thrust into the crime center of America, it was just that there were some people my parents didn't want us to know and a lot that didn't want to know us. For one thing, we were still considered "white trash." We were poor and from Texon. That was all it took for the others to label us, and for a nine-year-old, enough to ruin any amount of self esteem she might have. Texon was not blessed with a hospital environment, but the friendliness of its inhabitants more than made up for its landscape.

It was a huge change for the entire family, not just for me. Like Texon, the few trees it possessed were low, twisted mesquite trees. Rankin also had the huge tumbleweeds, and we were bothered by them more than ever because we had farther to walk to school. We even saw it rain dirt for the first time. There were very few rainstorms, and occasionally it would drizzle while the dust was blowing. The product was huge clumps of "rain dirt." One distinct difference in the surroundings was that there was not an oil rig in sight. Those rigs were in the many oil camps which surrounded Rankin and were largely responsible for its income.

None of the homes looked alike, and there were definitely different ranges of income. Our family was at the bottom of the social scale, except, of course, for the blacks and Hispanics who lived across the railroad tracks. That was another difference from Texon. There, we had all lived beside one another, regardless of race or income.

Rankin was much larger than Texon. It had a population of about 1,400. The children who lived in the oil camps close by came to Rankin in order to attend school. Rankin was still as dusty and windblown as Texon, and there were just as many tarantulas to count. Our school was only a 1A, but it had a lot more money than most schools its size because of the oil money with which it was supported.

I was envious of the oil company children from the first day of school. They had a special bonding similar to the one we had in Texon. I would miss that closeness they had the entire eight years I lived in Rankin.

My father worked as a maintenance worker for the hospital during the first part of the day. Then he cleaned the County Courthouse in the afternoon. My mother worked in the cafeteria for the school in the morning and for the hospital in the afternoon. My father would usually clean the hospital, come home for dinner for an hour, then go to the courthouse to clean it, and finally get home about eight o'clock. Both my parents were pushed pretty hard, and we were on our own a great deal of the time.

It finally dawned on me how poor we actually were. We couldn't see either Mother or Daddy anytime we wanted, like when we could just walk into the grocery store. We moved into a small two bedroom rent house. All three of us girls had to sleep in one bedroom, and Mother and Daddy in the other. I remember hearing my Mother and Daddy arguing a lot about money. That was also new.

In Texon, I couldn't remember them ever arguing in front of us. In fact, they were often openly affectionate. "Edward, I don't know how you can say that we can continue to put money aside for the girls. We're just going to have to wait a while until we're back on our feet. Cheryl has already been looking for a part time job close enough to school where she could work. Besides, I don't like to see you working yourself to death. This is as bad or even worse than the farm."

"I don't see how you can say we can't keep putting money away, Emma. Cheryl will be going to school in two months, then Annie. We can wait a while for Marcie, but that's all. I'll just have to work a few more hours, and we'll have to cut back on expenses." And that was what we did, because my father was still the head of the family, and he did practically work himself to an early grave to provide for us.

We girls got to wear even less store-made clothes and more handmade, unfortunately, by my mother. She should have sold her sewing machine and put the money in the bank. We wouldn't have minded in the least. There were a lot of times when there was no meat on our table, not because it was considered healthy at the time, but because we simply couldn't afford it. It was also necessary that we pay rent in Rankin, which was an additional expense for our family. I wished many times that we could go back to Texon, but it never happened.

We were at the bottom of the economic scale, and that seemed to contribute more to my natural shyness. Now that I think back, I must have been the most *naive* person ever born. How could people who belonged to the Rankin Country

Club have been so uppity to us? You'd think they belonged to Dallas Country Club! I guess it's true that what people think of you is usually what you think of yourself. The image I had of myself was an uncoordinated, poor, ugly geek. So you can imagine why I was so unpopular. I couldn't even make friends with the other kids who bussed in from other oil camps. They each had their own *cliques* and weren't inclined to include me.

Mother and Daddy both tried to boost our egos and moods. I remember how downtrodden that house was for a long time. I wanted a cat, but I knew that was impossible because Annie was allergic to cats and got hives. Daddy came home with two goldfish in a bag one day and put the bag in my hand. I remember exactly what he said, "These goldfish are your responsibility. It'll be fun to feed them, and they're really pretty!"

BIG DEAL! I never have liked fish, unless you can afford one of those huge two thousand dollar aquariums. So I pretended they were sick and flushed them down the toilet. Then I felt like a murderer for days. I could just imagine God putting down two or three bad marks under my name. I'd get to heaven, and St. Peter would say, "Are you the same Marcie Fitzgerald who killed those two fish in 1959? Sorry, that makes too many bad points. You go down to eternal damnation."

What I did next to try and make up for this blunder, was to go down the block where I heard that the family on the corner owned a baby alligator. Baby alligators were popular in the late fifties and early sixties. I asked Nancy, the girl who had the alligator, if it was expensive to own one. She said *no.* Since she was older than me by one year, and was an alligator *owner,* I believed her.

I had a little money saved up from my allowance and when Nancy said, "I'll sell you this one for a dollar cause my mother doesn't like alligators," I reasoned it was my only way to get on the good side *upstairs*. So, I went for it.

When I got home, Mother was cooking dinner. I said with great aplomb, "Look what Nancy on the corner just sold me. It was only a dollar. It's a baby alligator." Mother took one look and made a very diplomatic decision. "Put it down there and show it to your father when he gets home."

Daddy came in, washed up for dinner, and sat at the kitchen table to eat. Finally, I mustered up the courage to say, "Daddy, do you remember about my fish dying? Well, Nancy sold me a pet for only one dollar. I paid her with my own money. May I keep it?"

"What kind of pet?" There it was, the question I most dreaded.

"A baby alligator. It's cute, look," as I proudly showed my father my newest acquisition.

"What happens when it grows up, Marcie? What do you do about it then?"

"Grows up?" In my haste to make up with Him, this was something I hadn't considered. "I don't know."

"Take it back to Nancy. Tell her she can keep the dollar and give her back the alligator. That dollar will teach you a lesson. Do it right after dinner." Daddy got up and that was the end of the discussion.

That was a very expensive lesson, but I couldn't stand to touch it anyway. It reminded me of bugs. A dollar meant a lot though. I could get into the movies for seventy-five cents, so a dollar went a long way.

Later that year, Cheryl went to college in San Angelo and rented a room from Aunt Bessie. She also worked part time for a dress shop there. San Angelo was only about one hundred miles from Rankin, so Cheryl came home on occasional weekends when she could hitch a ride or afford the bus fare. Sometimes Aunt Bessie would bring her, and Aunt

Bessie would sleep on the couch.

The only motel in Rankin was unlivable, to say the least. The times that Aunt Bessie was there were the best times of all! I think though that Aunt Bessie loved moving to San Angelo. I had always thought of her as terribly old, but she must have been only about forty years old at the time. When she visited us, she and my mother would sit up talking for hours. My parents must have felt as unsettled as the rest of us.

Annie told me that Aunt Bessie had a boyfriend, but told me not to say anything because she overheard it, so naturally the first thing I said when she came to visit was, "Annie says you have a boyfriend. What's his name? Is he handsome?" Both mother and Aunt Bessie shot Annie a killer look. I loved it and couldn't imagine what the big secret was. After Annie finished strangling me when we went to bed, she told me Aunt Bessie's boyfriend was divorced. I said, "So what?"

Annie said, "I don't think Mother believes he's divorced, and that Aunt Bessie's just saying that because he's only separated. Daddy told Mother if she said anything to us, he'd kill her. He said it wasn't any of our business."

I wasn't sure I understood; I was pretty slow. But it didn't matter, because Annie said if I *ever* said anything about it again, I'd live to regret it. I think that was a real threat, and I believed her. Apparently, Aunt Bessie and her boyfriend went out for a long time. I'd hear her and Mother talking about him at night when she came for a visit. His name was Fred.

Having a smaller house also made my compulsive cleaning much easier, except when Cheryl came home on weekends from college. Then the house looked like a cyclone had just come through! She and Annie were still my idols. Cheryl was smart and popular, and Annie was smart, brave, and popular. So far, at least, my only assets seemed to be my constant cleaning and making good grades. I have always been too shy. Making new friends was hard for me, especially after the hall monitor problem I had experienced in Big Lake.

I started fourth grade in Rankin without knowing any other girls my age. It was a terrible time for me because I had no friends. I can remember one boy from Texon who moved to Rankin, and I had a huge crush on him until I graduated from high school. His name was Mark, and I tried every trick that I knew to make him notice me, but it was no use. He liked me as a friend. Mark always had someone else he was interested in. I think he should have told me when we were in the seventh or eighth grade that he would never be my boyfriend. That would have saved me a lot of grief. The cow eyes I shot in his direction had to have been obvious.

About a third of the way through the fourth grade, I finally met a girl my age that I liked and who liked me, although her family stayed in Rankin for only three months. They lived on the same block as we did, so I naturally tried to make friends. It wasn't easy. I now think that Amy must have been living in an alcoholic home, although I had no idea what that meant at that age.

My mother always tried to discourage me from going over to Amy's but finally allowed me to have dinner with her and to go to the movies. Amy's parents were very undependable and became angry for no reason at all. Amy invited me for dinner, and her father was supposed to drive us to the movies one Sunday afternoon. Not only was there no dinner, her father suddenly became ill and couldn't drive so we decided to walk which was completely forbidden by my parents. Everything was fine while it was still daylight, but we didn't realize that while we were watching the movies, it was getting dark outside.

We came out of the movies and really panicked! Naturally, I reacted with a clear head, "My mother is going to kill me! I'll never be able to go anywhere again as long as I live. We just have to walk home in the dark!"

It seems so silly now, but we were terrified! You would think we were walking through Central Park at midnight or in the wilds of Africa. Amy and I imagined all sorts of evil people and animals lurking behind bushes and houses. After all, I was now in the big city of Rankin and didn't know everyone the way I did in Texon. We got to the top of the hill where a little café was and I went in and asked the lady if I could call my mother.

My father came after us. First he drove Amy home. Then after we got home, he talked to me in the living room, "If you *ever* even consider lying or disobeying us, and especially walking around in the dark, I will ground you until you're 20!" I was grounded for a month. My mother was furious, too. I think the fact that we were no longer "one big family" like we were in Texon had finally sunk in. Maybe my parents were as nervous as I was. I was forbidden to play at Amy's house ever again, but she could come to my house occasionally, at least for the three months longer that she lived in Rankin.

Another odd thing happened that first year in Rankin. The black children went to the same school as we did. It was so amazing to me because I had never even *known* a black person until then. I didn't know at the time that I wasn't even supposed to play with them, even talk to them. I learned later that if I did, I would immediately be socially ostracized. Since I didn't know anyone and considered myself a nerd anyway, I talked and played with them whenever I wanted. I'm glad now that I did.

I was so confused about why the rules had been changed, but I was also hoping that the little black girl I saw crying on the bus in Big Lake was now sitting anywhere she wanted on the bus. I also hoped that she was going to school with all of the other children in Big Lake. That mean bus driver was probably still making her sit in the back seat. I would have loved to see his face when he was told that he could no longer make the black children sit in the back of his bus.

    I still didn't have any friends to play with in the fifth grade, but the most amazing thing of all happened that January. Kelly Roberts and her family moved in the house across the street! Mr. Roberts brought the playhouse with him, and he had even added some things to the kitchen. I thought that he would be nicer to Mrs. Roberts now, and I suppose he was, for about three or four months, until he beat her again.

    I know the police got involved somehow because Mrs. Roberts ended up in the hospital and almost died from a very cruel beating. Since Mother worked at the hospital, she was aware of the seriousness of the situation. She had the children stay at our house for about two weeks, and I was absolutely forbidden to visit them anymore if their father was there. Their grand-parents came to pick up the kids one day, and they stayed together as a family I guess. All I know is they moved out of Rankin that year and I never heard from Kelly.

    There I was, no friends again, and I was so jealous of Annie because her best friend, Erin, had moved just up the hill from us. Of course, I never had a best girlfriend anyway, since Marie considered me to be socially inferior. Annie and Erin sometimes made a very *dangerous* combination, so I was ON THE ALERT! They were both sixteen when we moved to Rankin, so they didn't have too much time to hassle me, thank goodness! I do have to admit though, that Annie started taking me to the movies without being asked and included me more often like a regular person. I guess she probably felt sorry for me because I hadn't made many friends, and those that I did make moved away.

Rankin had a downtown theater and a drive-in theater on the outskirts of town. When I realized there was a drive-in, I knew Annie would be making me hide in the trunk, and she did. However, I knew that there was no such person as a "ticket policeman". I was still very nervous, but I knew that I had better not make Annie mad. She hadn't lost her "revenge skills" just because we now lived in Rankin.

I didn't see very much of my father those first few years because he was working all the time. My mother's jobs in the school and hospital cafeterias kept her away about ten hours every day. I like to think maybe she was relieved that I had been born such a *cleaning nut* because she didn't have the time nor energy to clean much around our house.

The rules were that every Saturday, Annie and I would clean the house from top to bottom. Then if Cheryl came home that weekend from college, we would clean again on Sunday night because things were in such a shambles when she left. She now reminds me of that *Peanuts* character who always has a dirty cloud around him. I think his name is Pigpen. Anyway, it's really odd because now Cheryl is the clean person, and I'm the messy one. I like it more now. It relieves me of a lot of responsibility. I must have looked awfully downtrodden that first year in Rankin because after we had been there for about six months, my mother picked me up at school one day. This was the first time for that. In Rankin, unless I bummed a ride from someone else, I walked home. I remember that afternoon like it was yesterday. Mother showed up and said she had a surprise for me, but that I didn't have to take the surprise unless it was something I wanted. She took me to the drugstore for ice cream. I was excited.

We went to the other side of Rankin and parked in front of a strange house, and guess what—there was poor, sweet, half deaf, non-rhythmic Mrs. Collins, my former piano teacher. Mother said, "Marcie, Mrs. Collins moved here just about a month ago, and she has offered to give you weekly lessons at a special rate. Would you like to do that?"

"Are you kidding? I'd love to! Thank you. Thank you."

The piano was something I could do that Cheryl and Annie couldn't, and I just loved playing it. It made me feel special—that I could do something that very few other people that I knew could. I still love it.

Mrs. Collins repeated quite frequently that I was the best sight reader she had ever met. I think the piano did a lot for my self-esteem. Mrs. Collins was excited that her "star pupil" was able to take lessons. I was and am still very good at sight reading, but can barely tell time, because, of course, neither could Mrs. Collins. It really didn't matter to me though. I would walk over to her house once a week after school and then walk all the way home. I got a lot of exercise during the time I took piano lessons. I also practiced a lot. I still didn't have a friend, and it relieved the boredom.

I started playing in church again, and the church in Rankin was much bigger than the one in Texon, so I had a bigger audience. I filled in when the real piano lady couldn't be there and sometimes played a special song. I felt more like I belonged in Rankin for the first time since we had moved. The church in Rankin had a complicated organ though, and I only tried it a few times before I realized that it was beyond my capabilities.

In high school , when the regular lady who played piano became ill, I took her place. My father was very proud that at least one of his daughters decided to play music. He told everyone he met that his youngest daughter played the piano at church. Yes, I knew it pleased him.

☆ ☆ ☆ ☆ ☆ ☆ ☆ ☆

During the summer, between my fifth and sixth grade, I sprained my leg while showing off. Erin and her family had rented a house on a hill, and our house was at the very bottom. I bicycled up to Erin's house to tell Annie that she needed to come home for dinner. On my way down, I decided to race with Annie and went faster than I ever had. Unfortunately, the cover was off the water meter in our front yard and my bicycle hit it, with my leg being stuck in the meter hole. Although it hurt, it was worth it. I *finally* beat Annie at something! That was in June. Mother and Daddy were really nice to me, bringing things home like ice cream and letting me watch anything I wanted on TV. Sometimes you just have to grin and bear it in order to win at something. I had to stop piano lessons for a while, except when Mother could find time to take me over to Mrs. Collins' house. I felt good having beaten Annie at anything, and it felt great!

Finally, I made a very good friend, Barry Wilson. We had been going to the Baptist Church in Rankin for about a month before I noticed that Barry was always sitting in the back pew by himself. I found out later that he sat in the back pew because he played Solitaire. Barry and I became good friends after that. He could always make me laugh, and there were a lot of times later that I needed that! After I taught him how to play gin rummy and he taught me how to play Hangman, we were always busy in the back pew of the church on days that I wasn't playing the piano. We even recruited other card playing church members. Too bad we were too young to organize a regular Friday night poker game.

One day I went over to Reverend White's house after I had been playing the piano for about a year because I had to ask permission to change the program. I was so shocked when he answered the door. He was drunk! I had seen very little use of alcohol except for television, but you would have to be blind to have missed it. His living room was turned upside down. There were empty liquor bottles everywhere and piles of newspapers. I told my parents, but I never heard what, if anything, was ever done about it. I know he was still there delivering the same dull sermons when I left Rankin.

I guess his heart must have been in the right place. He obviously needed help, but alcoholism in the 1950's and 1960's was still considered a moral issue rather than a disease. He was probably doing the best he could under the circumstances.

In the seventh grade I fell in love for the first time, except of course for Mark. But Mark didn't hold a candle to Mr. Walsh, the new teacher. It didn't matter that I was only twelve years old and my object of desire was thirty. Every girl in my class was in love with Mr. Walsh. All of us thought he looked like a combination of Paul Newman and Frankie Avalon. I was over the baby stuff, like Captain Kangaroo and Roy Rogers. I was in the real world now, and I had a king-sized crush on my teacher.

It was on the first day of school that Mr. Walsh said he didn't believe in homework. The man was not just good looking but my kind of person. He was as handsome as Superman and was kind too, like Clark Kent! He had every student in his classes wrapped around his finger. I must have spent at least two hours every night on homework. He just didn't call it that. He called it "special attention," and we fell for it hook, line, and sinker. Mother commented, "I thought you weren't going to have to do any homework. That looks like homework to me." In Mr. Walsh's defense, I replied with a firm, "No, it's just special attention."

Boy, were we ever stupid! I learned a lot from Mr. Walsh. He always encouraged the ones who made the extra effort, and I did because it made me feel smarter. He had divided his class into three parts, according to their academic capabilities. I was in the highest, and I always worked hard to please Mr. Walsh. He always gave us papers to write, and that was my favorite part.

That was the same year I felt sick when nobody else was home. I called my mother, told her about my stomach ache, and she told me to take a square of the *ExLax* in the medicine cabinet. I thought she meant the whole square, not just the little divided part. What I took was equivalent to about ten times the recommended dosage. We only had one bathroom, and I think I occupied it for about three days. I had never been so miserable in my life. Of course, Annie had to change her mind about being nice to me and proceeded to tell everyone she knew about it.

Annie always knew when to choose the right moment to really get to me. Erin picked up the slack and once again I was the laughing stock of everyone in school. Thank goodness they didn't blab it to the kids my age. I still didn't have any friends. That's okay, though, because I also know when to pick my moments.

During the first year of the girl's basketball game in the high school, I helped to spread the rumor about Annie picking up the basketball like a football. Revenge can be sweet if taken at the right time. I kind of felt a little guilty about it though, because Annie couldn't help it that she was also bad at sports. That just made matters worse. However, Annie bounced back with her usual resolve. She always had friends because she was funny and not afraid of anything.

I suppose Daddy realized about that time that I was really lonely. He started getting home a little earlier on Saturdays, which meant that he had to get up earlier that morning. He would come home and take me "mountain climbing." There are no mountains in Texas, only hills, but we called it "mountain climbing" just the same. I loved it. We didn't talk much. We just walked around and looked at things. Every once in a while, we'd see a snake. Boy, that scared me. Daddy tried to tell me the snakes we were seeing were harmless, but I didn't care. Snakes are snakes, and I don't like them.

Sometimes we would take a snack and sit on the top of a "mountain" and talk a little bit. Daddy would ask me how school was going and if I had made any friends.

"School's okay, but the only friend I have is Barry Wilson. You can't talk to boys about everything. We really only talk to each other before or after church (Of course I left out the card part). Mark's here, but he's gotten kind of snobby."

I remember Daddy saying, "I like Barry's family. Did you know that his mother is very sick? She has migraine headaches. Your mother told me that several doctors have her on medication and warned her about her high blood pressure. She spends a lot of time in bed."

"No, Barry didn't say anything. I wonder why?"

"Maybe he didn't know what to say. Sometimes it's hard to talk about things like that. Anyway, they're a nice family. If you would like, you can invite Barry over."

I didn't tell him that the reason we were such friends was because we played cards in the back pews of the church. But I liked Barry out of church, too. He was kind of an outsider like me even though he lived in Rankin his whole life. We were both always trying to fit in but never quite succeeding because we were both extremely shy.

"I hope you realize, Marcie, that your mother and I want the best for you and your sisters. We work to be able to send you to college so *you* nor your sisters will ever have to cook in cafeterias or clean floors. We want something better for you."

The hill climbing almost became a weekend ritual, so much so that I looked forward to it every weekend. One day, Daddy suggested that I invite Barry along. I did, but he had to stay home. His mother was sick again. She died of a stroke the year after I graduated from high school.

Daddy often talked about what I was going to do after I graduated. My automatic answer was that I was going to college and maybe become a teacher.

Daddy warned me, "College is going to be entirely different, Marcie. There will be many different kinds of people there for you to make friends with , and you'll probably have to find a part-time job to help out, like Cheryl." What Daddy didn't realize was that I wouldn't be sorry to leave my friends in Rankin because I didn't have any to leave, except for Barry.

It was during the Kennedy administration that I decided I wanted to join the Peace Corps. The whole Peace Corps volunteer notion kind of relates to my need to be "saved" several times a year. It seemed so glamorous to go out to needy places in the world and be a combination Florence Nightingale/Mother Theresa-type person. When I realized that those "needy" places didn't always come supplied with exterminators, electricity, and inside facilities, I wasn't quite so eager. I did teach Bible School every summer, so I rationalized that I was doing my good deed, and I enjoyed teaching Bible School. Probably if I had tried harder, I could have been a good teacher.

It was in the eighth grade that I babysat for a new couple in town. They were both teachers and had two little boys. I was so shocked when I went over there. The only furniture in their house was a kitchen table and four chairs. Every other room was full of Playboy magazines. This was about 1962, and the parents were really hippies. I think they were disciples of Timothy O'Leary. Those two little boys were also the biggest brats I had ever seen. That was the last time I babysat for them. They had probably used every single girl in town before they moved because no one would ever babysit more than once. I'll wager that their two little boys must have been pretty screwed up when they got older. Their parents had a lot of growing up to do themselves.

Nine

    I finally met a good girl friend sometime in the eighth grade. Her name was Pam Pearson, and she was very pretty; shiny black hair, big brown eyes, and an olive complexion. She was one-fourth Indian. Pam was also one of the most intelligent and bravest people I have ever known. She had polio when she was very young and spent one year in a hospital, but that didn't stop her from doing her best. She became head twirler in high school, took dance lessons, and even ran track. She also said she planned to be a doctor.
    This was during the time when female doctors were almost unheard of, but Pam did become an anestheologist. I think if it hadn't been for Pam, I wouldn't have had any friends. I learned from her the courage to be more outspoken.
    I was jealous of her popularity, her looks, and her clothes. I don't think her parents were rich but I know they had a lot more than we had. Along with Pam came all of her adoring fans. It made high school more fun for me. I have no

idea why someone as popular as Pam thought I deserved to be her friend. She kind of reminded me of Marie.

Pam and I had a pact. She cut up all the frogs and/or bugs in biology labs for me, and I wrote English papers for her. I always tutored in English grammar anyway, and sometimes when the teacher had to leave for some reason, I was always left in charge of the class. English just kind of always clicked for me; science was a complete mystery.

I didn't learn very much in Biology, especially since Pam did most of my dissecting. Our science teacher died of a heart attack halfway through our junior year, and the football coach took over the class. Pam would have done a far superior job. She knew more about it than he did. I have always disliked science courses, probably because I never understood them. Maybe it would have helped if I had done my own lab work—what a unique idea!

Pam also loved to read and she introduced me to the world of reading. I practically lived in the library after that. Everyone we knew thought that *The Carpetbaggers* by Harold Robbins was racy. For a while, Pam and I went to the library and read all the sexy parts because the librarian, Mrs. Morrison, wouldn't let us check it out. Mrs. Morrison also didn't like having us hanging around, but that was her fault. Had she let us check out the book in the first place, we probably wouldn't have been there every afternoon.

Anyway, after we finally finished *The Carpetbaggers*, I started reading anything I could get my hands on. Reading began to replace my lack of friends. I have absolutely no doubt that it made a difference in my education, and I have Pam to thank for that, among many other things.

That was also the same year we had a homeroom teacher who reminded me a lot of my Grandmother Molly simply because she was just as crazy. Her name was Mrs.

Turner. She felt it was her duty to inform all the girls in her classes how to do makeup and hair and decorate their future homes.

At least once a week, Mrs. Turner would lecture us on proper behavior, "Under no circumstances should you place a person's photograph anywhere other than the bedroom. You should stick with one color scheme throughout the house, keep a clean house, serve nourishing meals, and *never* should you invite a male into your home when you are alone." Weird, huh? It's like you're ashamed that you have friends and family, so you have to hide their pictures in your bedroom.

It was highly apparent that Mrs. Turner dyed her hair jet black and wore a ton of makeup. She showed the required film to the girls which explained what she called "the monthly cycle." All of the girls in my class already knew exactly what "the monthly cycle" was from experience, but that never stopped Mrs. Turner. Yes, she and Grandmother Molly would have gotten along very well. They both had a few loose screws, although Mrs. Turner didn't use snuff.

I'm reasonably certain she smoked because there were stains on the fingers off her right hand and she often took a package of *Sen Sen* from her purse and sipped at the packet. I'm almost positive that she *entertained* male guests without a chaperone. She lived right across the street from us, and I was privy to a lot of information.

Unfortunately, the eighth grade was also when Mother started getting sick. I don't remember all the details. I think the rest of the family was trying to protect me because of my age. Mother had surgery that year. Annie and I went to the hospital to visit her. After about thirty minutes, she made us leave. She said laughing made her stomach hurt. She was out of the hospital and back to her jobs within a month. It took an awful lot to keep my mother down. Maybe that was the reason I didn't realize that she was so sick, or I didn't want to face reality.

Mother began having more sick days though, and a few trips to the doctor in San Angelo in addition to the one in Rankin. She started to lose a lot of weight, too. Anyone could tell that she was getting sicker.

She started coming home from work earlier and taking naps occasionally, and if I were home, I would always ask if I could take a nap with her. Of course she said yes, and those memories have always stayed with me. Mother would stroke my hair and call me her pretty baby. I never will forget it.

Daddy worked more hours to make up for the time that Mother couldn't work. I honestly don't know how he did it. I guess it was because he loved us all so much. No, he never told us but he showed it. He told and showed my mother how much he loved her.

That was also the year that Annie graduated from high school. It had always been school policy to have a Senior trip involving at least two overnight stays. But Annie's class ended that custom for everyone else. Annie and some of her friends sneaked out of the motel rooms and guess what? They went to a POOL HALL! They also went swimming, somewhere to eat hamburgers, and just generally goofed off. My parents were informed by the school that Annie had participated in the escapade and should be punished. I think Mother and Daddy just threw up their hands at that point and declared a stalemate. Annie never did do anything "bad", just a little adventurous

☆ ☆ ☆ ☆ ☆ ☆ ☆ ☆ ☆

Erin's parents decided to move to Goldwaithe about six

months before Annie and she graduated. Annie begged my parents to let Erin stay with us so she could graduate with the rest of the class, and my parents relented. Having both Annie and Erin in our house at the same time provided nonstop laughter. They should have "gone on the road" with some of their material. I remember coming in the house and finding Annie, Erin, and my mother in hysterics. My mother never would tell me the jokes. She said I wouldn't understand. I probably wouldn't have.

Unfortunately, Erin also got *pregnant* about a month after her parents had moved. My mother was so upset. All she could think about was the fact that Erin got pregnant at a time when she and Daddy were supposed to be taking care of her and watching her every move. Well, they apparently missed at least one very important move—or move*ment*!

Naturally, the school had to be informed. Rankin's policy in the 1960's was not to allow any pregnant girl to graduate with the rest of the class. Erin graduated but was not allowed to participate in the ceremony. It amazes me that the school would think that Erin would be a bad influence on the rest of the school if allowed to take part in the ceremony. It was as if they thought Erin would infect the entire class with her immorality.

This was also the year that the Beatles were coming to the United States. They were going to perform on the *Ed Sullivan Show.* Everyone I knew was excited. We all had some of their records, and Laura's parents even allowed her to have a "Beatles party." Again, my timing was a little off. Earlier that day, I was admitted into the hospital with acute appendicitis. They operated on me about ten that morning, and my mother and I watched the Beatles on television that next night.

I was disappointed at the time, but since then it has become a very special memory to me because I saw the program with my mother, whom I am positive would not have watched it otherwise. Then we napped together, and it was one of the few times that I remember being with Mother by myself and having her undivided attention. It brought back memories I had long forgotten, of when we would go on family trips, and I would lay my head on her lap. That made me feel more loved than anything she could possibly have done. During depressing times of my life, I try to remember my mother's hand that touched me with unconditional love and devotion. It still comforts me after all of these years.

Mother continued to get sicker. She had another operation in San Angelo and another one followed in Rankin that same year. Daddy, Annie, and I stayed with Aunt Bessie in San Angelo when she had her operation there. I remember walking into Mother's hospital room and being completely shocked by her appearance. There were tubes everywhere. I didn't realize or at least admit to myself until that moment how sick Mother was.

When the doctor scheduled my mother's next operation in Rankin, he asked for blood donations. The problem was that Mother's blood type was rare, and the hospital couldn't find anyone in Rankin with the same type. Mother remembered Aunt Bessie had the same type, and my father called her the next morning.

It was summertime, and I was still asleep when I heard the knock on the door. I very grumpily got out of bed and answered the door. There was Aunt Bessie!

"Hi, sweetie. I'm here to help while your mother is in the hospital. I have to go to the hospital first. Why don't you get dressed, and then I'll take you somewhere and buy you a good breakfast? I'll be back in about an hour."

When Aunt Bessie got to the hospital, she went directly to the nurses station and gave some blood. Then she walked into Mother's room with a huge bouquet of flowers. "I hope you realize this, Emma, but now that I have given you my blood, you're going to start smoking and swearing and God only knows what all. I hope that Edward warned you about that." Aunt Bessie told me that Mother started crying because she was so happy to see her. She took me up there later that day, and I was totally shocked. Mother was so yellow it reminded me of the swing set that Benjamin and I had painted. Again, she had tubes everywhere. It was then that Aunt Bessie told me that Mother had cancer. I was so upset that Aunt Bessie had to hold my hand practically all night. Annie was just as upset I'm sure, but she was trying to be stoic because she was the oldest at home.

After two weeks, Mother was released from the hospital. She was too sick to work. When Daddy told us that my mother would not ever be going back to work, I realized she was dying. Only that could make her stop pushing herself so that we could save some money. Neither of my parents wanted any of us to become a cook or a janitor; they wanted *better* for us.

Mother, even though feeling weak and in pain, cooked wonderful things for us, like blackberry cobbler, homemade rolls, and every kind of pie and cake you could imagine. I guess she was trying to show us how much she loved us. We would all try to keep her from doing any housework, but she did it anyway. One day she was vacuuming and fell and cracked her hip. Daddy took her to the hospital, but the doctor said that in her condition, it was unwise to operate. All we could do was to try to make her comfortable. After that, she spent a lot more time in bed.

There were a couple of times I would come home from school and hear Mother crying and in pain, "God, please just let me die. I wish I would just die." I was so shocked that I went out and sat on the front porch and cried my heart out. I couldn't believe this was happening to us.

Daddy was struggling to pay the hospital bills. The insurance Mother received through the hospital said that she had a pre-existing condition and refused to pay any of the medical bills. The hospital automatically enrolled her in the insurance five years before. There was no way that her condition was pre-existing.

Daddy was unfamiliar with attorneys and didn't know how to fight a large corporation. He just paid the bills as best he could but they were eating up that college fund for me and Annie that my parents worked so long and hard for.

During my freshman year in high school, I decided to try the speech team simply because Pam and Barry were on it. I really didn't have many interests, except for the piano. Our speech coach, Mr. Monroe, turned out to be one of the best teachers I ever had. He had so much ambition for us that even though we were a 1A school, he arranged for us to go to the 4A and 5A school speech meets. I helped with the research involved and worked hard at trying to speak in front of the other kids. I was scared and I was awful. Mr. Monroe took pity and from effort alone, he let me go as an alternate to the first speech meet that year in Midland. It turned out that I got to compete in extemporaneous speaking, and it was like a light bulb suddenly turned on in my head.

I found that I could speak in front of strangers, and that I also had the ability to research and remember material. The judges gave me a second place medal for extemporaneous speaking! I must have had the dumbest, most shocked expression on my face when I walked up the aisle to receive the trophy. The only person more surprised than I was Mr. Monroe. He knew my mother was ill and called her to tell her the good news. When I got home, Mother and Daddy were so proud of me. I never will forget running in the house, and they held me till I couldn't breathe.

Mother had my favorite chocolate cake already baked, and I think that except for the third grade play, that was the first time I noticed that Daddy looked really proud of me, too. He didn't say anything, but I could tell from his expression that he was pleased. I continued UIL speaking until I graduated.

Mother's condition worsened, and we were constantly trying to lift her spirits. One day Annie and I came home with a miniature dauchsund puppy. Sad Sack died two years earlier, of old age I guess. This little puppy was cute and playful. Mother absolutely adored that dog. For one thing, he kept her company while we were at school and while Daddy was working. Mother named the dog Friskie, and he doted on her. Soon they became great friends.

Friskie had this habit of running around with his nose close to the ground. It was funny because his ears were longer than the rest of his body and invariably became scratched and bleeding. He wouldn't raise his head in order to protect his ears, so we had to put bandages on them. Even Friskie possessed the Fitzgerald stubbornness.

Cheryl married later that year. She met Larry in Lubbock, Texas, where they were both attending Texas Tech University. They had a church wedding in Rankin. Cheryl started teaching the following September in a school about an hour's drive from Lubbock while Larry finished getting his degree at Texas Tech. A year later, Cheryl became pregnant. I remember vividly that Mother was visiting Cheryl when she started having morning sickness. When Mother came home, she announced, "I think Cheryl's going to have a baby. I hope it's a boy. We need a boy around here so your father and Larry can defend themselves." Cheryl called about a week later confirming Mother's suspicion. She was due in

September. I hoped it would be on my birthday!

That December, Daddy and Annie went out of town two weeks before Christmas and came back with a big package for mother, which they set under the tree. Annie told me (after days of coaxing) that it was a slip. Talk about disappointed! I couldn't imagine such a long drive just for a slip!

When Christmas Day came along, Mother opened the box and saw only tissue paper. Deep underneath all the paper was a tiny jewelry box. Mother opened it, and started crying. It was a gold wedding band. All these years she wore a thin silver band that Daddy had given her when they first married. It had worn so thin it was barely noticeable. Daddy said, as she held the band in his hand, "Emma, I promised you the day we got married that I would replace that little band with something better as soon as we could afford it. I know that it's been a long time, but will you please take this now? I love you." Then he put the ring on her finger.

I've never seen my mother so touched. She cried and hugged Daddy. I'm wearing that wedding ring now, and I wouldn't part with it for anything.

I asked Annie why she told me that the ring was a slip. She said because I never could keep a secret, and this was a pretty big secret. I suppose she was correct.

Cheryl had a little boy the following September whom she named Kenneth Edward. Mother died in April and didn't get to see him. I know that Cheryl was grateful that Mother at least had learned of the pregnancy before she died.

Mother had been painfully ill for so long, it was a blessing that she wouldn't hurt any longer. I didn't realize how much I would miss her until she was no longer there.

Mother died quietly in her sleep at home. Daddy came in to wake Annie and me to tell us that she was gone. I remember asking Annie what "gone" meant. Annie replied,

"He means that Mother is dead."

There were many people who admired and loved my mother, and the church was barely big enough to hold everyone. It was so strange because the day after Mother passed away, so did Friskie. The dog wasn't ill, didn't have an accident, we never knew what happened other than the fact that Friskie loved Mother so much. Maybe it *is* possible to die of a broken heart?

Now it was time for me to grow up. Actually, it was finally time for a lot of us to grow up. We no longer had my mother's strength to bind us.

We noticed something different about Daddy over the next few years. Annie and I assumed it was senility and grief. He started forgetting things and losing his temper for no apparent reason. Sometimes he would just sit in his chair, not paying any attention to us at all. This was in 1965 and before there was a great deal known about Alzheimer's Disease. He worked as hard as ever and came home every night, but he was even quieter than before, his driving became worse, and he was constantly forgetting things. His temper became increasingly worse and Annie and I were afraid to talk to him. He would burst into tantrums for no particular reason. It was as if he were a different person.

I felt I had lost both of my parents when Mother died. My father must have been even more lonely. Daddy had not only lost my mother, he also lost a great deal of the contact he had with the entire world around him. He could no longer express himself properly, nor even think in the same manner as he had before her death.

Annie stayed home a year after she graduated to work as a secretary at the high school. Daddy didn't have enough money to help her with college expenses because he was trying to pay Mother's hospital and doctor bills, and keep us eating regularly.

    Annie saved her money. The following year she moved to Lubbock to attend Texas Tech, with the help of government loans. Annie knew that a college education was the only way she would ever improve herself. It only proves that if you want something badly enough, and if you are willing to work for it, things have a better chance of working out.

    I have never forgotten that it was Annie who stayed home the year that Mother died. I know I couldn't have handled being alone with Daddy during that first year. And, it was still difficult doing it the last two years of high school.

    I was totally envious of the other girls my age who still had mothers. Cheryl was teaching school and had her own family. Being alone with Daddy for two years, without a doubt, were the worst of my life. I felt more alone, scared, hurt, and desperate than I could ever recall.

    Cheryl and Larry asked me to come live with them in Sundown so I could graduate there, but I felt Mother would have wanted me to stay with Daddy. I also didn't want him to live alone because he wouldn't be able to take care of himself.

☆ ☆ ☆ ☆ ☆ ☆ ☆ ☆

    It was a hurtful surprise when not one single person came by to ask if I needed anything. No one even stopped by from the church that we had so faithfully attended. There was one particular family who lived behind us that Mother had befriended. She would babysit, cook, and was just a friend to that mother. She never came over to offer condolences or to ask me if I needed any help.

    I have heard that people handle grief in different ways. I hope that my parents taught us to handle it in such a way that they would be proud, with a Christian heart and spirit.

Had we still lived in Texon, things would have been different. In Texon we were all one big family, ready to help each other. But not in Rankin. In Rankin, we were just another poor family that mattered to no one. And, at 15-years old, I was suddenly thrust into the job as homemaker, student and caretaker for my father.

I came down with a serious case of the mumps during my senior year. Dr. Major warned Daddy that it could be very dangerous for me to get out of bed and walk around. I remember Daddy coming home every day at lunch and warming chicken noodle soup. Then at night he would warm *more* chicken noodle soup. I lived on chicken noodle soup for weeks! The thought of chicken noodle soup makes me ill to this day, except that it reminds me that my father loved me and took care of me when I was sick. He remembered to come home to check on me at a time when it was difficult for him to remember much.

Being sick that week accomplished another special thing; I made a new friend, Brandy Moore. Brandy moved to an oil camp close to Rankin at the beginning of her freshman year in high school. Brandy, was immediately popular—and beautiful, with long blonde hair and big green eyes. She made the cheerleading squad her first year and in her sophomore year she was *captain* of the cheerleading squad.

We had some classes together but it wasn't until I got sick that we became friends. Brandy skipped lunch and brought my homework to me so I wouldn't fall too far behind. We became friends then and remained friends until this day. Brandy now lives in Nevada but we call each other often and have long telephone visits. I wish she lived closer.

☆ ☆ ☆ ☆ ☆ ☆ ☆ ☆

Daddy became stranger by the day. Finally, I asked Dr. Major if there was anything physically wrong with Daddy. He thought Daddy was suffering from Alzheimer's Disease and explained the symptoms. They fit Daddy like a glove. When I left the doctor's office, I had the weight of the whole world on my shoulders. I didn't know how to go on.

One of the things that bothered me was that Daddy refused to let me drive the car. Not having this transportation made it difficult to go grocery shopping. I was lucky, however, that Rankin wasn't *that big!* As it was, I had to buy groceries with the small amount of money Daddy gave me and then push the cart all the way home. The store was twelve blocks from our house, and I kept the cart at home. Daddy must have thought we were buying groceries in the 1940's because he never gave me enough money, which meant I would have to go more than once a week. It was good exercise.

It was then that Daddy started bringing food home that he bought from the hospital. He thought our grocery bills would be cheaper that way. He insisted I use these items, such as huge amounts of powdered milk, instant mashed potatoes, and cans of fruit. The canned peaches were the worst; they never tasted right.

Of all the things Mother taught us, cooking was not included, and now, I needed that training most of all. So, I stumbled along, preparing tasteless food. The only thing I cooked well was fried chicken which we ate often, along with those instant mashed potatoes.

☆ ☆ ☆ ☆ ☆ ☆ ☆ ☆

Since I had almost no experience in driving a car, Drivers Ed was not easy for me. It was a horrifying ordeal. I felt useless. I nearly flunked the easiest class ever offered in the history of Rankin High School. Everyone begged not to have to ride with me. This was probably because I almost had an accident every time I got behind the wheel. Mr. Wallace, the driving instructor, was always a nervous wreck when we even *approached* the car.

It was humiliating for me not to be able to drive, even in Rankin. In Rankin, you almost had to *ask* for a wreck to happen! I did, however, pass the written part. When I showed up to take the driving test , the police officer asked for my learner's permit. I told him I had forgotten it but he let me take the test anyway which I surprisingly passed.

As time passed, Daddy's condition grew worse. He acted as if I was only in the house for the sole purpose of cleaning, cooking, and shopping. That didn't boost my morale at all. My self-esteem plunged to its deepest in years. I needed to feel some sort of purpose to my life. Maybe that was why I tried so much harder in my speech efforts. It became a habit to stay longer in the afternoon to work on the speech files so that I could postpone going home to an empty house. Barry always stayed, too.

Speech competition gave me an excuse to get out of town for a couple of days. When I did well, my opinion of myself raised. When we went on our first speech meet, it was the first time I had eaten in a real restaurant. I was so impressed by Luby's, but determined to not let anyone know.

The only thing at that time that interested my father was my report card. I usually made all "A's" but when a few "B's" crept in, it upset him. Daddy never punished me though .I needed a show of love and affection but Daddy just wasn't the type. I never felt so abandoned in my entire life. I needed desperately for someone to wrap their arms around me like my parents had before Mother died.

I often wondered whether I was being punished by God

for something I had done. Gone forever from me were my mother's sense of humor, her caresses, the naps I would take with her, and her desire to learn about school and my friends. Daddy's few conversations with me were welcome, no matter how short. I missed those mountain climbing expeditions too.

For a while, I even felt abandoned by God. It sometimes occurred to me that perhaps Daddy felt the same way, not only because of Mother's illness and death, but because of his own sickness and apparent lack of friends. It never occurred to me until much later that he must have been becoming increasingly more confused and that, even withstanding my young age and immaturity, I could have been a friend to him as well as a daughter.

Ten

During my junior year Pam and I became best friends. Her friendship often made things better for me. Her parents gave her a Volkswagen for her birthday and she faithfully came by every morning and picked me up for school.

Mrs. Collins, my piano teacher, died from a stroke that year and I think of her often. I never fail to remember her when I play the piano, mainly because I still can't read the timing. I will always miss her, and I have enjoyed the piano all of my life.

During my last two years of high school, I developed an "Annie" streak. Maybe I was just trying to get noticed. Our class gave the Spanish teacher a nervous breakdown during the first semester which required internment in an institution. The school finally found someone in Rankin with a degree to come and babysit our Spanish class. The new teacher didn't know a word of Spanish.

Our chemistry teacher died from a heart attack in December, so the football coach took over. None of the students learned anything about chemistry that year, and we missed our real chemistry teacher, Mr. Winslow. His class was difficult but he took a true interest in teaching us. The football coach was no match for him.

Our algebra teacher managed to stay until the end of the year, but he left, telling us in no uncertain terms, that he never intended to teach school again. We tried valiantly to rid the school of its entire high school faculty, except for Mr. Winslow, but without success. We still had English, history, and homemaking with which to contend.

There was a boy my age named Harold who just fell in love with chemistry, no matter who the teacher was. He courageously tried to perform experiments at home and blew up his garage during an experiment involving a bomb. He was forever coming to school with scorched eyebrows and hands. I often wonder if he ever applied his scientific curiosity in college. I hope so.

Do you remember Etta Stone, Marie's sister from Texon? She and Cheryl kept in contact, so we learned that Etta married my algebra teacher, Mr. Wolfe. I recall Cheryl telling us that the last time she saw Etta and Mr. Wolfe, he was working for an engineering company in Midland. He must have really meant it when he said that he would never teach again. Just imagine—we actually made him change his profession because we were so mean to him. I think I recognized a fellow *victim* and closed in for the kill. The rest of the class just followed my shining example. Maybe that was my niche. Perhaps I should have become a Marine with basic piano and speech skills.

The class I enjoyed most was English. We had an

English teacher I liked but for the life of me I can't remember her name. I became her "right hand." I tutored, and I took over when she couldn't be there. It definitely was my best class.

Homemaking was one of my worst classes. Our assignment at the end of my senior year was to make a dress. We were supposed to model the dress at some Ladies' function in Midland when we were finished. I picked out a pretty blue material at the dry goods store in town. The pattern was a nice, simple A-line shift with long sleeves. It was part of the "Easy to Do" Simplicity line. They lied! It was most definitely not easy for *me* to do. Maybe it was easy for them to do. They just sat around all day and made patterns.

When I finished my dress, the right arm came straight out in front where the breasts were supposed to be. I don't remember how I managed to dress myself, and I never did know why it happened. It remains one of those great mysteries of science—like The Black Hole. I was working on it in Homemaking class, and after I realized what happened, everybody started laughing. Even Mrs. Davis, our teacher, laughed until she cried.

I pretended it was some sort of joke, but noticed one very important thing; if I tried hard enough, I could be the class clown. Being the class clown would at least make more friends for me. I had to stop and think though, did I want friends that much to make a buffoon of myself all the time?

Pam took the dress over to her mother to make the necessary adjustments. We all laughed about it. Pam's mother was nice enough to fix the dress and I made an acceptable "B" in class. I never wore the dress because it still looked awful. The only way that dress could have been wearable would have been to start over.

I faked a pretty good case of the flu on the day of the

trip to Midland. I suppose I carried the bad seamstress gene, so what could I do but accept my fate? I still don't sew a stitch. There went another burgeoning career down the drain.

It was during that year that I saw Marie again. Remember her? That snotty little girl back in Texon who always told her mother to tell me she wasn't there when I came to visit. I don't guess I liked her anyway but she was the only girl my age to play with.

Marie joined an acting group in Big Lake, and they came to our church to perform a program for Christmas. I will never forget how she treated me. I walked up to congratulate her and to say "hello." She looked at me and simply turned around. She couldn't have mistaken me for anyone else. She was just ashamed to be in my company. I was not sure if I could ever forgive her for that.

That same year, Pam took me to Merle Norman's in Midland for a make over. It was my birthday present from her. On my way home, with my fresh makeup, I knew that Mark would be impressed and fall hopelessly in love with me. When he saw me, he asked me what happened and told me I should go home and wash that awful makeup off my face. That was when I fell "out of love" with Mark.

I spent most of the summer between my junior and senior years with Cheryl and Larry in Sundown. I have often thought that it had been very selfish of me to leave Daddy alone, but I suppose I was in my "selfish teenage" period. I helped Cheryl with her baby. His name was Kenneth. He was one of the funniest babies I have ever been around. We tried incessantly to make him say "Mommy or Daddy or Aunt Marcie."

On a shopping trip we made to Lubbock, I was holding him in the back seat of the car, and he had been crying for about fifteen minutes. Running out of patience, I finally asked,

"Kenneth, would you please just be quiet for the rest of the way?" He immediately said "Okay." We couldn't believe it! The first word out of his little mouth was "okay." After that, we couldn't get him to stop talking. He never learned to master "Aunt Marcie" and called me "Ninny." That was very thoughtful of him.

☆ ☆ ☆ ☆ ☆ ☆ ☆ ☆

My senior year was full of surprises. Daddy started disappearing right after lunch on Sundays. I had no idea where he was going every week until one day Pam came over and while we were riding around town, we passed the small nursing home and saw my father's car in the parking lot. I couldn't imagine why his car would be there. I don't know how many times I tried to ask him about it, but he just ignored me.

The answer came within two days when , Mrs. Abrams, the manager of the nursing home, called the house and asked for Daddy. When I told her he was still at work, I asked if I could take a message."Would you please tell Edward that Mrs. Johnson will not be here for the next two weeks, so there isn't any reason for him to come by, unless he would like to. We always enjoy his visits."

I didn't even know a "Mrs. Johnson," so I asked as diplomatically as I could why Daddy had been visiting her?

"You don't know, dear? Your father has been coming by at least once a week, hoping to help Mrs. Johnson come out of her shell. She played the piano at her church in Big Springs before she moved in here. Before your father began stopping to visit, she just sat in her wheelchair and stared out of the window. Your father brought her up to the reception area and he played the piano and sang some hymns. Before long, Mrs. Johnson joined in. It's done her a world of good.

She now asks us to bring her back occasionally so she can play even when Edward isn't here. He has just been working miracles with her. We all told him that we hope he won't stop coming to see us. There are others here who could profit from his experience. He enjoys music so much, and our patients respond to him because of it. He seems like such a nice man. Would you please give him the message?"

"Yes, ma'am, I will. Thank you for calling."

I was speechless! Daddy playing and singing to help someone he didn't even know. Music helped bring Daddy out of his shell, at least at the nursing home. When he came home, I gave him the message. He said "thank you" and that was the end of the conversation. I don't know whether he ever went over there again. I hope he did. He needed friends and something to make him feel worthwhile.

It astounded me that Daddy took that kind of interest in the patients at the nursing home. It was admirable, but odd. Why was it that he never related to me, his own daughter? I discovered later that someone at the church suggested that he go visit the nursing home, maybe because they thought that was where he needed to be.

Perhaps he realized that they needed help and related to them because of their closeness in age. Maybe I should have asked Daddy to play the piano with me since music was one thing we had in common. It also occurred to me that Daddy had a really good heart. As much as he was suffering, he took his precious time to help someone else. Not many people can profess to that. I think Daddy had won his place on the "Good" side of God's tablet and would, someday, be in heaven with mother.

☆ ☆ ☆ ☆ ☆ ☆ ☆ ☆ ☆

The rest of my high school days were spent in a blur taking care of the house), staying after school to work on the speech files, being the editor of the school yearbook, and keeping my grades up. Sometimes I felt like a child playing house because I was shouldered with what I considered to be adult responsibilities.

Unlike Texon, in Rankin we had to keep our doors locked and I was invariably locking myself out of the house. Daddy finally gave an extra key to Mrs. Turner across the street in the event I locked myself out again. It didn't take me long to remember my key, because whenever I was forced to ask her for it, she would keep me inside lecturing constantly about how to run one's home properly. I felt like saying, "Look, I'm seventeen years old! What do you expect?" Of course, I never did. I just remembered my key more often.

My senior year I went to state in ready writing, extemporaneous speaking, and Barry and I teamed up in debate. That time was special. We worked on our files for weeks. We continued practicing on the way to Austin, and then just started laughing. There wasn't any more research we could have done. It was always like that with Barry—a lot of work and laughter mixed. Without a doubt, Barry and Pam were my best friends. We could work and laugh together about almost anything. What I didn't realize was that "true friends" are always hard to find at any age.

Barry and I won first place in debate. I also placed third in extemporaneous speaking and third in ready writing. Barry placed third in poetry, and Pam placed second. We worked hard for those medals, and everyone was proud of us, except for my father who never said one word to me. I'm not sure he even knew anything about it.

Our speech group helped perform a program close to the end of our senior year. Barry and I wrote it all, and we attempted to make it humorous. The entire speech group performed every act, so Barry and I also acted. It was a lot of fun. I never mentioned any of this to Daddy because I didn't think he would remember or particularly care, but I was so wrong. When I came home that night, Daddy was waiting for me, much like he and mother had after my first speech tournament. Daddy had secretly gone to the program and waited for me to come home. He told me how proud he was of me for writing a lot of the program and for my acting. I was stunned! It was at that moment I realized that perhaps I should have given Daddy more credit for at least trying to be an important part of my life. He had been as lost and confused as I.

☆ ☆ ☆ ☆ ☆ ☆ ☆ ☆ ☆

The highlight of my senior year was when our speech team went to Lubbock, again competing with all of the bigger 3A and 4A schools. We took the school bus, spent the night, and everyone but me went back to Rankin before the awards were announced. I stayed behind with Cheryl and Larry because Mr. Monroe asked me to pick up any trophies we had won and let him know later that day. I knew we had done well, but didn't know *how well* until the next day.

I spent the night in Sundown with Cheryl and Larry and Cheryl drove me back to Lubbock for the awards presentation. It was only 30 miles away. We arrived a few minutes late and sat at the back of the auditorium, which was literally filled to the brim with hopeful winners. I was scared to death.

Cheryl said, "Don't worry. Whenever they call your name, just stand up and walk down there like it was exactly what you expected to happen. This is your day, Marcie."

That day really *was* special. What Cheryl and I didn't know was that every single person from Rankin who had competed in the meet had won at least one trophy. Rankin won a total of **sixteen** trophies, some kids winning more than one. Each time a name from our team was called, I walked down that long aisle to get the trophy. Four of the trophies were mine! I should have brought my shopping cart!

After a while, the audience started clapping and cheering whenever I got up. I tried to remember what Cheryl said, and I finally just started smiling every time I walked down the aisle, which was a distinct accomplishment for someone as shy as I. I wished with all of my heart that Mother were there to see me. Maybe she was there that day after all, clapping just as hard as anyone and trying to make me feel worthy of something I had done.

Finally, I had proven that I not only belonged in Rankin, but that I had a talent for something special. I felt at that moment that I had learned to communicate with others, and if I worked hard enough, perhaps I could use that talent later in my life. Nothing since has ever made me feel as successful or praiseworthy as that day.

The presentation lasted only about two hours, but it seemed as if it took an entire day. I wish it had. I called Daddy that night and told him about the trophies. He told me he was proud of me. He'll never know how much I needed to hear that.

When I graduated, Annie, Cheryl, and Larry came for the ceremony. I won a small scholarship, but all I could think of at the time was that if I had tried harder, I could have probably been class valedictorian or salutatorian. I had been excusing myself from applying harder because having to take care of my father. Apparently, I had become effective at feeling sorry for myself. Daddy and I had become adept at excluding others and we both had been living in our own special world.

☆ ☆ ☆ ☆ ☆ ☆ ☆ ☆ ☆

We pulled up to the entrance of the dorm. There were a lot of other parents with their daughters, helping them take their things up to their rooms. I looked around and noticed that many of the parents were trying not to cry. They were all hugging and kissing their daughters. I missed Mother all the time, more so now.

Daddy and I got out of the car, and he took my things from the trunk and set them down on the curb. Then he stood very rigidly in front of me, and announced, "Marcie, I hope you realize that you can no longer come back home. This is your home for the next four years. I don't want to see you again until you've graduated."

Then he got in the car and drove away. I hadn't expected a hug or kiss from him, but he just told me he didn't even want to see me again! I felt like bursting into tears, but repressed them. I didn't want anyone to notice, so I turned and started taking my luggage upstairs. There wasn't much to take. The only way I was even able to attend school was with Mother's social security checks and financial aid.

I finally put everything in my room and sat on my bed with my knees curled up, still trying not to cry. I missed my mother so much, and I missed Daddy like he was before he got sick. A girl walked into my room and introduced herself as Patsy. She was my roommate.

"Was that your father downstairs? I wish my parents had just dropped me off. I get so tired of them hanging on. Mother especially." When I didn't answer, she kind of shrugged and went out in the hall in search of other potential friends.

I couldn't answer her because I was so close to tears that if I opened my mouth, they'd start flowing. I was *really* feeling sorry for myself. All I could hear out in the hall were parents trying to help their daughters get settled and saying their goodbyes.

I opened my suitcase. There was a Bible in it! It was Mother's! I picked it up and brought it to my chest as tears rolled down my cheeks. A picture fell out! It was my graduation picture!

I opened it to put the picture back inside and, on the first page, I saw an inscription. The handwriting was shaky and hard to read, but it said, "I love you, Marcie. When you get lonely, open this book and remember your mother and me. All we ever wanted was for you to have a better life than we had. Study hard." It was signed "Daddy."

I ran through the open dorm door and down the hall and looked out of the window, There was Daddy, sitting in his car looking up as if he could see me. I could see tears running freely down his face.

I'm not certain whether he saw me or not and I just stood there clutching the Bible with tears rolling down *my* face. I desperately wanted to run down there, throw my arms around him and hug and squeeze him and tell him how much I loved him. I wanted him to know that he had fulfilled his every promise to me and my sisters against tremendous odds.

I almost gave it all up then. I didn't need school. I wanted to go home with him and take care of him. He was my daddy and he loved me more than I had ever realized. I had no reason to ever be jealous of anyone again. My Mother and Father sacrificed *everything* for me and my sisters. I was one lucky human being!

Yes, it finally dawned on me why he'd been so harsh when he was telling me goodbye. He was trying to tell me that he wanted me to stay in college and not come back to Rankin to take care of him. It must have been as hard for him to say as it was for me to hear the words. I wanted to run down there and hold him with all my might, but I knew he wouldn't like it. If only he had kissed me goodbye and told me he loved me. I wished that I had been more understanding and realized that his leaving me here was as difficult for him as it was for me. I guess this was the only way he could say goodbye. I no longer cared what anybody thought. I stood there crying aloud, with my palm against the window, wishing I could touch him. I wanted so much to tell him I loved him, that I understood. Then he pulled away, heading for home.

I went back in my room and sat there holding Mother's Bible as close to me as possible. When I looked around the room, I realized that this was exactly what she would have wanted. Not for Daddy to be sick, but for me to be sitting in a dorm room, ready to start college. The last of her "babies" was prepared to start something that would result in an easier and better life.

From that moment on, whenever I felt discouraged or lonely, I took out Mother's Bible and held it. Until this day, I often recall Daddy's face as he sat there in his car looking up at me. He had given me a gift that was both precious and unselfish. I had never in my life loved Daddy more. Down deep inside, he really was the same man who sat with me those Saturday afternoons when we climbed mountains together and talked about when all of us would be leaving for college. Through his gift of Mother's Bible, I also felt her presence more strongly than ever. Thank God for them both.

EPILOGUE

We all loved Texas. Cheryl taught school in Sundown, until she and Larry moved to Abilene where Larry worked with his father in a small independent oil firm. Cheryl and Larry had one more child, a boy named David.

They divorced two years later and Cheryl went back to teaching, eventually earning her master's degree. She married Paul Wilson about ten years later and they moved to Beaumont. Paul had two children by a previous marriage and the combined families have become one.

Cheryl became so proficient with computers that she gives seminars nationwide on the use of computers in the classroom.

☆ ☆ ☆ ☆ ☆ ☆ ☆ ☆ ☆

Annie received her degree at Texas Tech and began teaching in San Antonio in 1967. She later got her master's degree at Southwest Texas State University in education. Always independent and adventurous. She went to work for the American Schools in 1976; they have schools all over the world. She has taught in Haiti, Bulgaria, Romania, Iran, Algeria, Brazil and Honduras.

Nothing has dampened her spirit or desire for adventure. In all of our hearts, Annie always has been and probably will always be, the little girl who broke into the pool hall in Texon. She never married but had numerous opportunities. She was a tough one to tame. Her constant companion is her cat, Peachy. She takes her everywhere she travels.

☆ ☆ ☆ ☆ ☆ ☆ ☆ ☆ ☆

Marcie obtained most of her bachelor's degree in English from Southwest Texas State University. Her schooling was interrupted by an early marriage and she had one daughter, Gaye, who is now attending Texas A & M University, majoring in Biochemistry with plans to become a physician.

After twenty years of marriage, Marcie divorced and went back to school to earn an associate's degree in Legal Assistance and certification in their national organization. She began a career in that field.

Marcie remarried in 1992, to a physician, James Lancaster. James had one daughter, Megan, who married William in 1995. Now, Marcie's daughter Gaye, her husband's daughter Megan, her husband William, and James and Marcie are one family. James and Marcie now live in Midland. Because of an illness, Marcie no longer works as a legal assistant and has pursued her lifelong dream of writing.

☆ ☆ ☆ ☆ ☆ ☆ ☆ ☆ ☆

All three daughters, Cheryl, Annie and Marcie, were born children of poor peanut farmers who bought a store in a Texas oil camp, Texon. Their parents, Emma and Edward, instilled in them the need of an education, love of family, a strong work ethic, and the Christian spirituality which has always been an important part of their lives. Although their parents are now with God, their spirit and memory will always endure through their children and children's children for generations to come.

They each feel that what they learned from their parents is available to all of us if we simply look beneath the surface. If we can, we're sure to find, as they did, **TEXAS GOLD**.

124   *Texas Gold*

The Whole Family in Texon

(Left to right) Emma and Edward Fitzgerald, Annie, Marcie & Cheryl

Marcie's 4th Birthday Party, Texon

Joyce Shaughnessy

Baby Annie and Cheryl
1947

Marcie, 1st Grade
Texon 1957-58

Marcie, 11th grade, Rankin

My father in 1977

Other Books by Swan Publishing

HOW NOT TO BE LONELY . . . If you're about to marry, recently divorced or widowed, want to forgive, forget or both, this is an excellent book to read. Candid, positive, entertaining and informative —a fun book to read with answers that will help you get a date or a mate. It tells you where to find them, what to say and how to keep them. (Over 3 million copies sold) . . . . $ 9.95

HOW NOT TO BE LONELY *TONIGHT* . . . The sequel for the *MALE* reader. Other than being courageous and strong, smart women want their man to be sensitive, caring, and understanding. "The" book to give to your man. Or, for men who really want to learn what turns the modern woman on . . . . $ 9.95

HOME IMPROVEMENT . . . This is Volume 1 and the first book Tom Tynan wrote on home improvement. It has literally **hundreds** of homeowner's most often asked questions, **answered!** In but 3 years it is in it's **eleventh** printing . . . . $ 9.95

BUILDING & REMODELING . . . If **you** plan to build yourself or have it done for you or remodel by doing it yourself or using a contractor, this book tells all. Plans, inspectors, inspections, architects, contractors, subs, **everything!** . . . . $ 9.95

BUYING & SELLING A HOME . . . Volume 3 by Tom Tynan, and it gives you the "secrets" of buying as well as selling a home. It is so thorough, informative and innovative, that thousands of Realtors have bought it to give to their clients. By doing this, they attest to the fact that the book is extraordinary . . . . $ 9.95

STEP BY STEP *15 Energy Saving Projects* . . . Volume 4, is Tom's newest book. Simple, safe, inexpensive, easy projects for the homeowner to save energy costs. Instructions for tools, methods and drawings for each. Energy companies all over the United States are buying thousands of copies to give to their customers . . . . $ 9.95

NEW FATHER'S BABY GUIDE . . . Another best selling book by Pete Billac. The perfect gift for ALL new fathers. There is not a book for new fathers quite like this one! Tells (dummy dad) about Lamaze classes, burping, feeding and changing the baby plus 40 side-splitting drawings by athlete/cartoonist Cash Lambin. Most of all, it tells dad how to SPOIL mom! GET IT for that new daddy! . . . . . . $ 9.95

YOUR FRONT YARD . . . A fun book of information by KTRH Gardenline co-host John Burrow, tells about plants, trees, grass, pesticides, fertilizer, **everything** you need to know to win have "the" best looking yard in your area. John makes this book for everyone to read. KTRH Garden of the Month contest . . . . $ 9.95

VEGETABLE GARDENING *Spring and Fall* . . . by John Burrow, is his newest book and tells everything a beginning gardener needs to know to grow a garden in the country, city, or in an apartment. A really great book! . . . . $ 9.95

ELVIS IS ON THE LOT . . . By Jim (Mattress Mac) McIngvale with Dave White, is the true story of how a couple invested $5,000 and became millionaires by hard work, advertising, a plan, perseverance and a goal. It has the formula about how you can do it too! It is a well written, excellent book to read and enjoy . . . . . . $ 14.95

HOW TO BUY A NEW CAR & SAVE THOU$ANDS . . . Inside information on dealerships and salespersons. This book by Cliff Evans, a former car salesman and general manager, really will save you thousands on your next new car purchase . . . . $ 9.95

A WOMAN'S GUIDE TO SEXUAL ENHANCEMENT. . . or **REVERSING IMPOTENCE** *FOREVER* . . . A truly great book written by two world famous urologists, Dr. David F. Mobley and Dr. Steven K. Wilson. This books tells MEN how they can *reverse* this problem but, men just aren't buying the book. The terrible thing is **not doing anything about it!** Included are many drawings which show how impotence can be reversed and is **perfect** for the woman to read, then "slip it" on her partners pillow . . . . $ 9.95

JOYCE SHAUGHNESSY is available for personal appearances, luncheons, banquets, seminars, etc. Call (713) 388-2547 for cost and availability.

★ ★ ★ ★ ★

Send a personal check or money order for $12.85 per copy to: Swan Publishing, 126 Live Oak, Alvin, TX, 77511.
Please allow 7-10 days for delivery.

To order by major credit card 24 hours a day call:
(713) 268-6776 or long distance 1-800-866-8962
Delivery in 2 to 7 days

★ ★ ★ ★ ★

Libraries—Bookstores—Quantity Orders:

Swan Publishing
126 Live Oak
Alvin, TX 77511

Call (713) 388-2547
FAX (713) 585-3738